SPTS

BLIND

Once again, Scott Morton has provided a great service to the body of Christ, especially to ministry leaders. Addressing the challenging and often fear-filled topic of fundraising, Scott's new book gives hope and help to many through his strong biblical and practical approach.

— **Betty Barnett**, author of *Friend Raising: Building A Missionary Support Team That Lasts*

Blindspots is a biblically-based, must-read for all ministry leaders engaged in fundraising. Scott Morton provides a wealth of practical principles, steps, and ideas for leading others through the challenges of funding a ministry.

— **Dave Blomberg**, Director and Ministry Partnership of Mission Aviation Fellowship

Blindspots is definitely going to bless any serious ministry leader.

— **Emeka Ohahuru**, City Director, The Navigators, Lagos, Nigeria

Many leaders do not know practical steps of how to help their people do fundraising well. Scott puts feet to admonition, know-how to necessity and fun and satisfaction to the process.

I often say this is a "must read" book. But *Blindspots* is a "must do" book. This is much more a book of action than information. Scott practices what he preaches. *Blindspots* has the smell of the fire of battle not just the musings in the closet of academia.

— **Jerry E. White**, PhD., International President Emeritus, The Navigators, Author of *Honesty, Morality and Conscience* and *To Be a Friend.*

Our blind spots — what a great perspective from which to share the many concepts, strategies, and views on fundraising and development! Scott's many years of experience and the situations he shares show he has been there and has led the way to finding his blind spots.

May this book help us all to find our blind spots, and work around or through them. Well done, Scott.

— **Dr. John R. Frank**, CFRE, Coaching and Consulting, Founder, Stewardship Summit

Blind spots indeed. Many years ago, as a young leader, I was tasked with supervising a self-support missionary, and I had little understanding of the whole funding process. This book would have been a godsend in those days, and today I am certain it will be an invaluable tool for non-profit leaders who lead self-support staff.

— **John Gilberts**, Chief of Staff and Director of Global Partnerships, Greater Europe Mission

Every non-profit leader should buy *Blindspots* and make it required reading by their leadership teams!

Leaders set the environment and tone of the organizations they lead. It's been my experience one of the biggest blind spots of non-profit ministry leadership is side-stepping the recruitment of necessary resources to accomplish the mission they represent. People take fundraising cues from the involvements of the top leader. So goes the leader, so goes the financial health of the organization. The leadership funding role is one that is often shirked, shuttled or delegated because a leader is fearful or feels that recruiting money is 'below the dignity' of the office they occupy. Morton takes this issue head-on with a biblical overview.

God has used Scott Morton to motivate, train, coach, and influence countless faith-based, non-profit organizations through his writing, training and personal ministry. I am one of those leaders. There is no one better qualified to speak to leadership funding than Scott.

The body of Christ will be furthered as leaders, including myself, take Morton's insights seriously.

— **Lauren Libby**, International President/CEO Trans World Radio

Scott Morton, in his usual down-to-earth, biblically-sound and practical approach, delivers yet another essential tool for every Christian worker and leader who raises support. *Blindspots* addresses the challenges that Christian workers face in a vulnerable and redemptive way that leaves you filled with hope. It is insightful, diagnostic, and practical. I highly recommend it to everyone who is engaged with the advancement of the gospel.

— **Nelson Musipa**, Zambian National Director, The Navigators

My wife and I have been on Scott's financial support team for many years. Scott definitely applies the funding principles outlined in the book. I vividly remember his invitation to become an "anchor donor." He described the financial "ask" he was about to make as an "obscene amount!" And it was! And we gladly joined up! We look forward to his email, snail mail, and personal visits throughout the year which keep us informed about his work in advancing Christ's kingdom.

— **A long-term giving partner of the Morton's from Chicago**

Scott Morton is an Ezra 7:10 man — He studies the Word. He practices the Word. Then he teaches the Word! Learn the biblical and practical how-to's of getting your staff and organization fully funded. He will help you identify the fundraising obstacles in your perspective and approach, then give clear and effective steps to overcome them. Personally, I need this book *right now*!

— **Steve Shadrach**, Author of *The God Ask*

The revolution of my poor view of fundraising came when I began to look into the Scriptures on the subject. Scott Morton visited Navigators of Japan to teach from the Scriptures what he is teaching in this book. I found that the Scriptures had plenty of teachings and case studies on the subject. This is where I felt I hit the goldmines.

— **Yuji Uno**, International Funding Coach, Navigators of Japan

Just as Scott's book, *Funding Your Ministry*, can transform your personal funding, *Blindspots* can transform your whole organization in overcoming the unnecessarily biggest obstacle in completing the Great Commission—money.

— **Jed Olson**, Fundraising Development Trainer, Youth With a Mission

Blindspots should be required reading for all nonprofit boards and staff. Fundraising blindsides so many nonprofit leaders and people raising their ministry support. In this book, Scott Morton shines the light on why we wrestle with funding — as individuals, as leaders, and as teams. He gives biblical insights and tools, stories, and strategies that will help you learn fundraising. As if that weren't enough, he writes to leaders in multiple countries, not just in North America. I am so glad Scott wrote this book. I know I'll be giving it to ministry leaders for years to come. Scott, I am being nourished reading the book. It is a gift. Thank you.

— **Marc A. Pitman**, CEO, The Concord Leadership Group

Scott's book *Funding Your Ministry* has been so helpful and loved here in the UK. Now Scott has brought his down to earth and biblical approach to help leaders be involved in encouraging their teams. This is such an important part of organizational fundraising. I am already excited about the impact it will have.

— **Gillian Dowse**, Navigators UK

Again, Scott Morton helps us with biblical and strategic guidance in fundraising. As the Senior Coordinator for the Lausanne Younger Leaders gathering in Jakarta — with participants from 140 countries — I witnessed how Scott Morton's funding kit gave hope and practical help to many. I pray that *Blindspots* will do the same with executives and team leaders involved in fundraising.

— **Ole-Magnus Olafsrud**, Navigators Norway and The Lausanne Movement International

As a local church global ministries director, I am often grieved when I see talented global partners defeated by what they see as the "funding giant." This book will encourage, challenge, motivate and educate everyone involved. In particular, this is a pioneering work directed at the role that executives and team leaders can and should play in ministries with deputized fundraising.

— **Herb Janes**, Pastor of Missions, New Hope Church, Minnesota

You are not alone if you are a leader who is timid about fund raising. Fund raising is a significant spiritual activity. It is a gospel activity. Thoroughly biblical and practical, Scott's insights will inspire you to move from, "I would rather others in my ministry raise the funds our organization needs" to "I want to be personally involved in fundraising and trust God for only what He can do for the sake of the Kingdom."

— **Ellis Goldstein,** Director, Ministry Partner Development, Cru

SP●TS

BLIND

Leading your team & ministry to full funding

Scott Morton

Forward by Mutua Mahiaini

BLINDSPOTS
Leading Your Team and Ministry to Full Funding

© 2016 Scott Morton

Published by CMM Press, the publishing ministry of
the Center for Mission Mobilization. mobilization.org

CMM Press
PO Box 3556
Fayetteville, AR 72702
cmmpress.org

Unless otherwise noted, all Scripture references taken from New
American Standard Bible (NASB) Copyright © 1960, 1962, 1963,
1968, 1971, 1972, 1973, 1975, 1977, 1995 by The Lockman Foundation

Blindspots is a resource of Support Raising Solutions (SRS),
a ministry of the Center for Mission Mobilization. SRS provides
training and resources to Great Commission workers worldwide
to be spiritually healthy, vision-driven, fully funded. Visit our
website for resources to aid you in raising financial
support for your ministry.

SupportRaisingSolutions.org

Printed in the United States of America

1st Edition, 1st Imprint

Dedication

For those gospel workers
whose ministry has been minimized
by poor financial leadership.
There is hope.

TABLE OF CONTENTS

Section 1

Section 2

Section 3

Section 4

Forward

AS LONG AS MONEY IS SEEN as unspiritual and fundraising as the unspiritual side of ministry, fundraising will always be considered a problem to be resolved instead of a wonderful privilege to be embraced for the sake of the gospel. Most leaders have spent very little time thinking about the honor of believing God for the funding of their ministry and the stewardship dimension associated with it. God has called Scott Morton to help gospel workers and leaders to address this anomaly and to bring a spirit of joy and freedom so that money can be the wonderful servant it was intended to be. The sad alternative in many people's experience is that money proves to be a terrible tyrant when it is viewed wrongly. This book addresses blind spots which are not innocuous. They hinder the advance of the gospel, and clearly Scott's motivation is to see the gospel of Jesus Christ advance into the nations. I have been personally blessed by Scott's ministry as he has coached me in fundraising and as he has influenced our entire movement to think biblically and practically about how to trust God and work towards full funding for the sake of the gospel.

I am delighted that Scott has taken the time to tackle this issue by taking the reader into the Scriptures. Many fundraising techniques are available in the secular world — and many work wonderfully — but we whose motivation is to advance the gospel of Jesus and his Kingdom have a huge advantage that has often been ignored. This book invites us to have our eyes opened and to experience fresh wind in our sails. Most leaders will find their questions and challenges reflected in the situations described in this book. I pray that the Lord will use *Blindspots* to bless and motivate many and to bring hope and success in an area that matters so crucially for the glory of God.

Mutua Mahiani
International President of The Navigators

Preface

SOON AFTER BECOMING STATE DIRECTOR FOR The Navigators in Wisconsin, I realized fundraising was a big deal in leadership. I was doing okay in raising my personal ministry budget, but my fledgling staff and interns were barely getting by. Though they never said a word about it, they struggled to have enough money to come to regional meetings, or fund the inevitable family emergencies. Our only sources of extra funding were the meager profits on our yearly weekend conferences.

My underlying value was: "Every tub floats on its own bottom." That kept our team from overspending, but it evolved into an every staff for himself or herself mentality — survival of the fittest. But I didn't see it. I was so blind, I didn't even help my Regional Administrative Assistant who struggled (with tears) to fund her position. I had a blind spot, two actually. I assumed:

- My staff could figure out their funding without my interest or participation.

- I wouldn't need additional money beyond my personal ministry budget.

I was wrong.

I wish I could have a do over on those early days. There were no books or seminars to guide young ministry leaders like me. But God had mercy on me and guided me to Philippians 4, where I learned Paul was not ashamed to receive gifts. I also found Exodus 18, where I saw that it was God who was the true Source, not people. In Luke 8:1–3, I discovered that Jesus had a funding team. Financial hope blossomed as I applied what I was learning.

As I took on more leadership positions, I realized fundraising problems frustrated all leaders. There were also systemic and organizational challenges, but no one addressed them. Something was wrong, and I was part of it.

Thankfully, I stumbled into exploring the fundraising practices of Bible leaders, looking at well known Bible stories through a different lens — money. How relevant were their stories? To this day I continue to study them, and I continue to discover new insights about how they dealt with funding issues. You know their names. You've read their stories. Now, allow these six biblical leaders to guide you through the blind spots of fundraising leadership:

- Moses — In his vision to build a godly nation, fundraising played a surprising role. His potential donors had no real jobs and they had already given to The Golden Calf Project. Time on the mountain with God taught him that fundraising is not a necessary evil.

- Joash — He was King of Judah, but young and inexperienced. He wanted to rebuild the temple, but his first attempt using professional fundraisers failed. So he took a hands on, simple action step, and it worked.

- Hezekiah — His people were not supporting the Levites (the Kingdom workers of the day) as God had commanded. His country was also under threat from Assyria. This King of Judah focused on what was important over what was urgent. Deliberately overlooking Assyria, he focused on fully funding his workers. The nation experienced a resurgence of devotion to God.

- Nehemiah — While in captivity in Persia (present day Iraq), he was saddened by the broken down wall and the spiritual decline of the Jewish people 700 miles away in Jerusalem. Books have been written about Nehemiah's leadership skills, but the key to his leadership success was a risky fundraising encounter.

- David — At the prime of his life as a powerful king, David made huge mistakes and suffered the consequences. He was passed over as builder of the new temple, but did not resign himself to despair. In his final leadership role, David modeled great generosity that influenced his colleagues to be generous also.

- Paul the Apostle — He was not silent about money. His challenge was teaching the new Christ followers to bring giving into their discipleship practice.

To lead well, you must address funding, both for you and for your staff and organization. Funding challenges will land on your desk sooner or later. I found that my Iowa farm common sense solutions were inadequate. And the historical Evangelical tradition that "speaking about funding is unspiritual" was discouraging.

These six biblical characters guided me out of many bad decisions and they are making me a better leader both in money and in non-money issues. They will pop up in the pages you are about to read, and you will get to know them better, not only as fundraisers but as godly leaders.

I have inserted a principle callout in most chapters, and in some chapters I include addendums of personal failures and "how I did it" solutions to give you examples.

Some of my frustrations with leadership and leaders seep out, that is by design. I did not sterilize this study because biblical leadership is not sterile, especially in money matters.

In the appendix are detailed worksheets that are ready for you to use in your leadership. You can download full size worksheets for your ministry at scottmorton.net. They will make you a better leader too.

Scott Morton
November 2016

Introduction

WHEN GIFTED, CAPABLE MEN AND WOMEN step into ministry leadership they get a surprise — fundraising! Maybe they saw the fundraising line item on the job description, but it was 'glossed over' in favor of more interesting leadership topics. Soon fundraising becomes a huge headache.

In driving a car we look to the front, back, and side to side, but every car has 'blind spots' — areas we cannot see. It is similar in leadership. Fundraising blind spots in leadership are invisible, and they cause even good leaders to make mistakes.

Leaders likely are well-trained generally, but in fundraising or creating fundraising strategies they are expected to 'figure it out.'

They look to consultants, seek board members' advice, or they try to delegate 'this funding stuff.' To no avail. Sadly, gifted, energetic leaders are minimized because of fundraising challenges thrust upon them, their teams, and the organization.

But here is hope! In this book I share my own blind spots in funding and those of leaders from around the world. 'The fundraising Goliath' (as my friends in Africa call it) is being defeated!

Rather than knee-jerk into pragmatic solutions, we'll start with the Bible. *Blindspots* comes out of my many years study of six Bible leaders who overcame the same financial issues facing you. It also comes from grappling with the raw, on the ground challenges faced by leaders from many cultures. It's not theory!

Whether you are responsible for 200 field staff in Sub-Saharan Africa, six campus reps in Kansas City, or two interns in Kuala Lumpur, this book will help you identify fundraising blind spots in your leadership and organization and will serve as your hazard map as you lead your team through the rocky terrain of nonprofit fundraising.

You: Blind Spots in Your Personal Outlook

As leaders, our opinions about fundraising are often based not on biblical principles but on our personal experiences with fundraising. I have heard leaders pontificate against mission workers raising support because of their own negative experiences in making 'asks' years before. Some leaders may even telegraph a "God is broke" mentality without realizing it. They think more about cutting costs than raising additional funding. These uninterpreted, often painful, funding experiences infiltrate our leadership decisions and even our leadership demeanor.

*Whether you are a young leader or experienced, the pressurized arena of fundraising will bring out the real you. Sooner or later—your personal blind spots in fundraising will pop up. Successfully leading a fundraising ministry starts with **you**—from the inside out.*

A leader's personal outlook on funding deeply influences his or her decision making. That is why we start with the Bible rather than pragmatic best practices. Are your unfiltered funding experiences shaping your opinions about fundraising? Will you allow the Bible to shape you?

1

Welcome to Leadership—Now Raise Some Money!

A FEW WEEKS INTO YOUR LEADERSHIP role you discovered that fundraising is a bigger part of your job than you thought — much bigger. Think back to your interview for this job. Did your interviewer point out the fundraising line item in the job description? Perhaps, but not in detail.

But today you get it. Of the issues lying on your desk and brewing in your mind, many deal with money — usually not enough of it!

Furthermore, you wonder if a scarcity mentality — the sad assumption that there is not enough money in God's universe for your work to thrive — like carbon monoxide is silently suffocating your staff. Avoiding deficit seems more important than expanding ministry. Cutting expenses seems easier than raising new money. Ellis Goldstein, Ministry Partner Development Director with Cru, says it this way:

"Instead of vision shaping the budget, the budget shapes vision."

On the other hand, idealistic young leaders sometimes go to the other extreme by naïvely assuming funding automatically appears at crunch time, every time.

It's not easy to lead in finances.

In Africa, ministry leaders nicknamed fundraising Goliath, taunting them from the opposite hill, daring them to attack. Like Saul's army, they faithfully put on their armor each day and shouted the battle cry, but they never attacked!

3

Why is Goliath not being subdued? Lack of vision? Lack of determination? No and no. The problem is fundraising illiteracy in leadership--Blindspots!

Promotion to leadership does not magically produce fundraising expertise. Most leaders are terrific in other parts of their job, but fundraising blind spots undermine their effectiveness.

Plus, leaders are often too overwhelmed even to think about fundraising until deficits pop to the surface. If only this money stuff could be delegated!

For perspective, you need to know that leadership fundraising dilemmas are not new. This classic quote is still relevant:

> *"Somehow, the business of raising money gets shuffled into the specialty area and is left to the development officer. The only time senior management tends to get involved is when deficits are cropping up and everybody is wondering why the organization isn't raising more money."* [1]

A few years ago I coached a young staff worker whose struggles show how leadership blind spots silently poison ministries:

M was an experienced minister starting a new work on a tough East Coast campus. No students responded to her team's surveys to start a Bible study; no one seemed to care. Finally she met a young woman who said, "Yes, I want to hear what the Bible says about spiritual life." They set an appointment for three days later at the Student Union. M was excited!

But she confided to me that she canceled the appointment. "Why?" I practically shouted.

"Because I didn't have $4 to buy her a Coke."

M confessed with tears that she had no money. She had squandered four weeks in July allocated to recruiting new giving partners. Tearfully admitting her mistake, she vowed to do better. Fine. Progress was made that day with this sincere gospel worker.

But as I drove away something was bothering me. I wondered: *Where was M's supervisor? Why was she left alone without accountability and shepherding during her futile funding attempts in July?*

And what about the National Office? Why do they allow staff to launch ministry without full funding? If there was a full-funding policy, why was it ignored?

This $4 Coke micro-event reveals a leadership problem —*your* problem — whether you are M's local supervisor, her Regional Director or National Director. The gospel was lost that day because of $4.

Sadly, stuff like this happens every day. As a leader, it is your problem. Own it! No need to be defensive. And you must not be 'philosophically neutral' for that communicates that you don't care. This can be solved.

However, you cannot solve it alone. M must think differently. So must her supervisor, her Regional Director and the National Office.

Where to start? Look below the surface to discover funding difficulties. When a staff or project is not fully funded, find out why! Even if it is painful, find out what's going on.

Consider my story: Early in leadership I considered my staff's funding to be *their problem*. I exhorted them to do fundraising, but I did not help them. I did not give them time off for fundraising. I didn't take time to listen to their fundraising emotions. I was wrong. Later, when I started showing a sincere interest in their funding, new lines of communication opened, and they began to succeed financially.

TAKEAWAY

* As a leader, are you willing to honestly look below the surface to find the real issues lurking behind funding problems?

* Are you willing to "own" your staff's funding challenge?

* Do you suspect a scarcity mentality has infiltrated your team? Do you have a scarcity mentality?

* Do you find yourself defensive when it comes to fundraising? Why?

- Do you find yourself "philosophically neutral" in fundraising?
- To whom will you turn for answers beyond your experience and expertise?

Is Fundraising a Necessary Evil?

MOST LEADERS ACKNOWLEDGE THE IMPORTANCE OF fundraising, but they secretly feel it is a *necessary evil* — like changing your computer password for the 27th time. However, this attitude telegraphs to donors that they are a burden. They might even pick up your latent resentment.

Let's look to Moses to escape this *necessary evil* view of fundraising.

During his 40 days on Mount Sinai, Moses was given the Ten Commandments to begin to build a nation. He was also instructed to launch a fundraising campaign! God told Moses:

> *Let them construct a sanctuary for Me, that I may dwell among them. (Exodus 25:8)*

Under God's direction, Moses exhorted the Jews to:

> *Take from among you a contribution to the Lord; whoever is of a willing heart, let him bring it as the Lord's contribution. (Exodus 35:5)*

Can you hear Moses's skeptical fellow Jews saying, "You spent forty days with God and this is the result — we give our stuff away? We're not rich, you know!"

But Moses' appeal demonstrates leadership. Months earlier God appointed Moses to boldly appeal to Pharaoh to let go of the Israelites so they could freely worship God. Now He appoints Moses to boldly appeal to the Israelites to let go of their possessions so they could erect a tabernacle for God's presence. Both of Moses' appeals were leadership roles. But one was fundraising — a necessary evil? No way!

Even more, couldn't the Creator of the Universe have miraculously built a tabernacle for His Presence without asking for the precious possessions of these Sinai survivalists? But God chose to give His people the privilege of being a part of His work. Moses was the holy intermediary to invite them to give.

PRINCIPLE:

Fundraising is not a necessary evil. It is a ministry of connecting the purposes of God with the people of God in voluntary giving.

God can fund His kingdom without our help. However, He chooses to make ordinary people His partners through giving. As we give our treasures, our hearts are drawn toward eternal things, and the bond of materialism is broken. As Matthew 6:21 reminds us: "Where your treasure is, there your heart will be also."

Fundraising is not a necessary evil. You are a holy intermediary, a matchmaker, to connect the intentions of God with the resources of the people of God.

Giving is an honor. Inviting people to give is also an honor. Calling it a necessary evil is blasphemous.

Now, a short but necessary sequel.

If you are a holy intermediary to connect the intentions of God with the resources of people, it is assumed you (like Moses) are listening to God. The question is:

Are you faithfully spending time alone with God?

Leaders who rarely meet with God on their own Mt. Sinai will struggle to confidently connect the purposes of God with the resources of people. You cannot separate fundraising and leadership from your walk with God.

A few years ago on a coaching phone call with Mutua, then a ministry leader in Nairobi and now International Director of the Navigators, I saw the importance of time alone with God. Mutua pointed out Exodus 25:40:

And see that you make them after the pattern for them, which was shown to you on the mountain.

Mutua said, "The leader is the servant of what he has seen on the mountain." Mutua had heard the impossible from God — an all-Africa conference for five hundred gospel workers. Cost? Only $300,000!

God spoke. Mutua determined to obey what he heard on the mountain! And that meant rearranging his schedule to embrace his fundraising responsibility.

Surprisingly, his efforts to raise $300,000 in America were dismal. It was then his wife Stephanie asked him, "Does God want this conference to take place?" Yes! That meant focusing on friends in Africa — impossible! Several counselors advised him to cancel.

But God spoke to Mutua out of Mark 8:4, the feeding of the 4,000. When Jesus wanted to feed them, the disciples asked, "But where in this remote place can anyone get enough bread to feed them?" (NIV) From a $300,000 fundraising point of view, Africa seemed like a "remote place." But Mutua kept going.

Finally, after many appeals across Africa, the $300,000 was raised — including a major air carrier giving an unprecedented discount for conferecs. And it started with Mutua hearing from God on Mt. Sinai.

But how do busy leaders find extended time with God? Stuff comes up, like your website going down and the web master is snowboarding in Peru, or unexpected visitors dropping by "just for a minute." As we become more and more busy we depend on old messages or old mantras rather than taking time to find a new word from the Lord — fresh manna. I confess I have arrived at my office "manna-less," having skipped my time with God because of an early morning meeting or being worn down from fourteen hour days. That's when Luke 5:16 encourages me:

But Jesus Himself would often slip away to the wilderness and pray.

Jesus, busy as He was, took time to be alone with God. So must you. You are a holy intermediary, the matchmaker. Like Moses, go to the mountain to hear from God *before* you appeal to people.

TAKEAWAY:

View of Fund Development

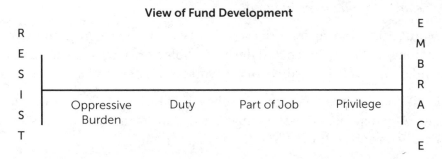

Analyze your view of fundraising according to this chart. Where would you place yourself on this chart? Where would you place your supervisor? Your individual staff?

- Are you allowing a *necessary evil* approach to fundraising to penetrate your leadership culture?

- What needs to change so you can spend quality time hearing from God—daily, weekly, yearly?

- What are you hearing from the Lord these days about your ministry? About your personal life?

What helps me:

I realize you work long hours, and I have just challenged you to make fundraising a higher priority. More bricks, less straw? No. I am not asking you to work harder, just differently. After years of too busy frustration, here's what works for me:

- I take two hours each Sunday afternoon or Monday morning to plan and pray over my week—a mini-Mt. Sinai visit with the Lord to listen for His voice.

- My planning is not done until I have finished my "do list" for the week, prioritized it and prayed over it.

- Then I ask this question: Are fundraising and donor ministry on my do list this week? For example:

  - Writing a thank you letter Monday

- Setting an appointment Tuesday with a major donor
- Scheduling a Friday thank you lunch with a key partner. When fundraising activities do not make it to my calendar, my stress increases.

Do You Hesitate to Talk About Money?

LEADERS TALK ABOUT GIVING MOST AGGRESSIVELY when they have a need. Except for giving campaigns or Stewardship Sunday, instruction on biblical giving is missing from our discipleship curriculums and the preaching calendar. The exceptions are the many pastors who teach from Malachi 3 about storehouse tithing every Sunday, but that is not the full counsel of God on giving.

In South Africa I gave a talk on biblical money management to an energetic group of young adults. I announced: "For the next hour we are going to talk about money and we are *not* going to take an offering."

The audience was stunned. Silence. Then cheers and high-fives broke out! Several came up afterwards and thanked me for not taking an offering. But one of the hosts asked, "With so many working people here, are you sure we shouldn't take an offering?" Hmmm.

Some organizations and churches take pride in "never talking about money!" My heart goes out to pastors who would love to teach biblical giving but have been shut down by well-meaning elders: "You'll alienate the parishioners!" they say. "Money split our church 30 years ago."

But silence creates two problems:

1. It sends the message that giving is not important except when there is a deficit or to build a building.

2. People will learn about giving from *somewhere*. If you don't teach them they are susceptible to "health and wealth" teaching or sec-

ular materialism! Orb they may assume tithing to the local church is all the Bible teaches about giving.

Can we get to the place where we teach giving as a part of discipleship, not merely because we need money? Mission pioneer to Brazil, Jim Peterson, said, "People need to give much more than I need to receive." That echoes Jesus' words, *It is more blessed to give than to receive.* (Acts 20:35)

PRINCIPLE:

Leaders must teach biblical giving as part of discipleship. Otherwise giving is perceived as optional or only for the super-commited.

The Apostle Paul was not silent about the discipleship of giving.

*But just as you **abound** in everything [faith, speaking, knowledge, zeal, love]...see that you **abound** in this gracious work [of giving]. (2 Corinthians 8:7, emphasis mine)*

"Abound" is *perissos* — to go beyond, super-abound, excel. *Perissos* described the large quantity of fragments left over when Jesus fed the five thousand.

Paul elevated giving to the same importance as faith, knowledge and love. He is saying, "Be as excellent at giving as you are in your other spiritual attributes." Furthermore, his frequent admonitions to do good deeds (Titus 3:14, Galatians 6:2) imply giving. Can you do good deeds and *not* give?

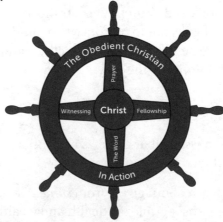

Perhaps you recognize this historical wheel illustration, which has helped millions. The spokes are not legalistic rules but spiritual disciplines to help us be like Christ.

- The word and prayer spokes help us relate to Christ (the center).

- The fellowship and witness spokes help us relate to people — believers and nonbelievers.

But let's draw in one more spoke — giving — how we relate to the things God has placed in our hands. God owns it all (Haggai 2:8), and we are stewards seeking to honor our Source. He is a generous giver; therefore, we are generous givers. Add giving to your discipleship teaching.

I love drawing the wheel with five spokes for giving partners. I use Luke 21:1–4 for the giving spoke, the familiar story of Jesus observing the rich men and a poor widow putting their gifts into the treasury. Jesus said the widow "put in more than all" even though she gave only two small copper coins. Why? Because "she [gave] out of her poverty [her living]" whereas the rich gave "out of their surplus." Jesus commended the widow because her giving affected her lifestyle. If we give only out of our discretionary income, we've missed the point.

I have spoken with mission leaders who admit their organizations have not taught giving as strongly as needed. Let's change that trend and teach giving *early* and *often*. Why?

- As in Paul's day, money shouts loudly for first place in our hearts.

- It has been documented that money is the most frequent subject of arguments in marriage.

- The world constantly tempts us to borrow money to buy stuff we don't need, and to believe we are owners rather than tenants.

- Biblical financial illiteracy is the carbon monoxide (unseen destructive force) behind many other problems — such as relationship disruptions, personal stress and business failure.

Martin Luther spoke of three conversions — head, heart, and pocket-book. Would Luther say you are truly discipled if you have not been discipled in biblical giving?

Giving must be taught as thoroughly as we teach other topics of the Christian walk, and not just when we need money. Start with the Bible study in "Appendix B: Creating Your Personal Giving Plan". Use it in small groups, in one-on-one discipleship, or to create a sermon or seminar.

Jesus spoke boldly and frequently about money. It is time we followed Jesus' example rather than listen to cultural sensitivities. Why are we so reticent?

TAKEAWAY

- What can you do to ensure giving is taught as part of discipleship in your ministry?
- Review the 4-spoke wheel diagram with your staff. Discuss what Scriptures on giving you would add for the fifth spoke.
- Draw a 5-spoke wheel with a couple of your giving partners. What is their response?

What helps me:

Over the years I have timidly approached teaching the discipleship of money. I was afraid people would think I was hinting for support.

Here are two approaches I take now in discipleship one-on-one meetings.

1. "Bob, what is a topic Jesus talked about frequently, maybe more than any other topic...money. Let's see what He said about it. And by the way, this is not a backdoor appeal for support!"

   Then I draw out the Wheel Diagram as above and insert a giving 5th spoke using Luke 21:1–4 or Luke 12:13–21 as the text. I dialogue over the text more than pontificating. I don't answer all questions but leave them wanting to know more.

2. "Bob, have you ever wondered about how to become poor? Let's look at what the Book of Proverbs says."

   Then I give them the "Appendix H: 60-Minute Proverbs Study" worksheet. I don't try to finish it all, but stretch it out to two or three sessions.

These sessions about the discipleship of money are well received! My fears were unfounded.

How's Your Giving?

IN GOD'S ECONOMY, HOW YOU GIVE directly impacts how you receive. Proverbs 11:25 says, "The generous man will be prosperous, and he who waters will himself be watered." Is it possible that your personal giving habits may silently be impeding your ministry?

The Apostle Paul taught the young Church principles for God-honoring giving. This is a good time to evaluate your personal giving practices with Paul's giving principles. Perhaps you'll find personal blind spots in your own generosity.

A. Give systematically.

On the first day of every week each one of you is to put aside and save, as he may prosper, that no collections be made when I come. (1 Corinthians 16:2)

The Greeks had a custom of helping those in need called *eranoi* — an informal association of friends who joined together to help, not with gifts but with interest free loans. [2]

Paul is not gathering money for a loan. Nor is he asking for a one time *harambee* — the lovely giving custom of East Africa employed at marriages, funerals, and emergencies. By exhorting new believers to set money aside weekly, Paul elevates the *planning* of giving. Biblical giving is not to be a spur of the moment decision based on what you have in your pocket. He wanted the Corinthians to think about giving all week long.

That was new to the Greek culture.

Do Christians today have giving plans? Most would say yes, sort of. But I find their plans are hazy, not written down, often not discussed with spouses. Turning in a yearly pledge for their church on Stewardship Sunday is not a complete plan.

Furthermore, believers often make giving decisions based only on what is in their purse rather than in their paycheck. They give out of cash on hand rather than their *increase* (Proverbs 3:9). Some clever Africans reduce cash in their wallets before church on Sunday so they can "give all they have" with a clear conscience.

Does Paul's admonition to plan your giving seem unspiritual? Shouldn't giving be *spontaneous*, led by the Spirit? Yes, but planned giving can be Spirit-led too.

Here is what Alma and I do as an example: Each January we forecast our income for the next twelve months and prayerfully discuss what we think by faith the Lord wants us to give each month. Our giving plan includes our local church, the poor, gospel ministries, and our family. Giving is a non-optional line item in our monthly household budget.

What about spontaneity? As part of our giving plan, we set aside a generous amount each month for spontaneous giving. If we don't give our spontaneous amount in the current month, we add it to next month. If we give beyond the budgeted spontaneous amount it doesn't reduce the planned amount already set. If our income goes down or if we receive an unexpected windfall, we adjust our plan.

And here's the key: We give first — before we spend it! Some Christians make commitments to support churches or missionaries, but what they mean is: I will give if I have enough left over after I have done my spending for the month.

Since it is God's money, honor Him by thinking through how He wants you to manage it. Flippant, thoughtless stewardship does not honor Him. When you borrow a neighbor's car, are you not thoughtful in how you use it?

Do both! Let the Spirit guide you in your planned giving, *and* let the Spirit guide you in your spontaneous giving. It's not your money!

B. Give proportionately.

Giving is "acceptable to what a man has, not according to what he does not have" (2 Corinthians 8:12). This corresponds with an Old Testament principle:

> *Every man shall give as he is **able**, according to the blessing of the Lord your God which He has given you. (Deuteronomy 16:17, emphasis mine)*

You can't give what you don't have. If your income goes up, give more! If it goes down, you are free to give less.

C. Give vertically.

Biblical giving is not merely a horizontal transfer of your assets to your church's balance sheet. Biblical giving is vertical. Notice the vertical Godward trajectory of these phrases from 2 Corinthians 9 (emphasis mine):

> *11 You will be enriched in everything for all liberality, which through us is **producing thanksgiving to God**. 12 For the ministry of this service is not only fully supplying the needs of the saints, but is also overflowing through many **thanksgivings to God**. 13 Because of the proof given by this ministry, **they will glorify God** for your obedience to your confession of the gospel of Christ and for the liberality of your contribution to them and to all...*

- *Producing thanksgiving to **God** (vv. 11–12)*

- *They [the receivers at Jerusalem] will glorify **God** for your obedience (v. 13)*

When I put my giving envelope in the offering plate at church, I visualize it ascending through the roof, through the clouds, all the way to heaven. When the ushers count it, they are puzzled. They ask, "How did this envelope get these smoky burn marks?" It's simple. Those are atmosphere reentry scorch marks. My gift has been to heaven and back.

D. Give cheerfully.

2 Corinthians 9:7 is a popular giving verse:

> *Each one must do just as he has purposed in his heart, not grudgingly or under compulsion, for God loves a cheerful giver.*

Cheerful is the Greek *hilaros* (English — hilarious). Sadly, many believers give with the same joyless enthusiasm with which they pay their electric bill. But why do they pay their electric bill joylessly? Since we are stewards of God's resources, every financial decision is holy — even the electric bill.

When Stewardship Sunday approaches, church members joke about feeling sick and not being able to attend. Sure, it's a joke, but what does it reveal? Instead, when the offering is announced at church, let's stand up and cheer!

Question: Have you noticed that Paul does not mention tithing? As a former Pharisee, he would have meticulously tithed even small garden seeds (Matthew 23:23). Why is he silent on tithing?

Can you imagine Paul saying to the new believers at Corinth, "You received Christ by grace, not by obeying the law, but in giving you must follow the Old Testament tithing law?" Unfathomable!

Suggesting that tithing is *not* the giving standard might contradict what you have been taught by well-meaning teachers. Isn't it odd that ministry leaders today teach what Jesus, Paul, and the early church patriarchs did *not* teach? Don't let 1,500 years of tradition distort the New Testament. For a full discussion on tithing, see "Appendix E: The Great Tithing Misunderstanding"

TAKEAWAY

- Do you have a giving plan that includes both spontaneity and planned giving?
- If married, are you and your spouse in agreement on your giving plan?
- Have you discovered the joy of giving?

Asking Others To Do What You Do Not

THIS LESSON COMES FROM THE FAMILIAR story of David's final act of leadership in 1 Chronicles 29, near the end of his life around 970 BC.

Despite bringing Israel to its high point as a nation and having accumulated great power and wealth, the aging King David had an unfulfilled dream — building a magnificent temple for the Ark of the Covenant, which still dwelt in Moses' 400-year-old tent (1 Chronicles 16:1). But God told David that because he was a man of war and blood, his son Solomon would build the temple instead of him.

Though surely disappointed, David nonetheless deliberately amassed huge amounts of building materials over twenty five years. Even though David would never see the new temple, he showed great commitment to the future by generously giving 3,000 talents of his *personal* gold and 7,000 talents of his *personal* silver — *over and above* the building materials he had already accumulated. This was his final and surprising act of leadership as he was ending his 'career.'

> *Moreover, in my delight in the house of my God, the treasure I have of gold and silver, I give to the house of my God, **over and above** all that I have already provided for the holy temple. (1 Chronicles 29:3, emphasis mine.)*

So how much did he give? 1 Chronicles 20:2 describes David's defeat of the King of Rabbah, whose gold crown weighed one talent. David gave the equivalent of 3,000 gold crowns. That's a ton of money in any country!

"Over and above." He could have been content with giving the national silver and gold he built up during his reign as king, but he also gave personally. And his personal giving influenced others. Responding to David's appeal to consecrate themselves and seeing his generosity, the tribal leaders also gave, and their combined giving surpassed David's.

> *Who then is willing to consecrate himself this day to the Lord? Then the rulers of the fathers' households, and the princes of the tribes of Israel, and the commanders of thousands and of hundreds, with the overseers over the king's work, offered willingly. (1 Chronicles 29:5b-6)*

PRINCIPLE:

Asking others to do what you don't smacks of hypocrisy and undermines your influence in their lives.

David's appeal and generous personal giving stimulated the tribal leaders to give. Following this example, church consultants urge pastors to be the first to give toward building campaigns and (like David) to tell their congregations how much.

Similarly, when I was asked to lead a capital campaign, I determined to be the first to give. Before the campaign was announced, Alma and I committed a three year stretch amount *above and beyond* our regular giving. Then, following David's model, I invited the board and national leaders to give "stretch gifts" before we appealed to others.

The application is obvious: Give generously to the organization you lead so you have moral authority to ask others to do the same. It is not enough to say that you give your time to your organization. That's your calling. David did that, plus he gave his personal resources.

If you do not give generously to your own organization, how can you ask others to give generously? I'm not suggesting token gifts! Your giving is an indication of how much you truly believe in your work.

Now let's go one step further. As David modeled generosity, his own staff (rulers of households, princes and commanders) also "offered willingly." How about your staff? Do they "offer willingly" to your organization?

Of course, do not make it a shame issue. The key word is "willingly."

David's staff didn't give out of coercion or shame. If your own staff do not willingly give financially to the work they represent, why not?

How about your board members? Since board members speak for your organization, they must also be givers. Even if you bring them on because of a specific non-money contribution, they should still give. But sometimes they do not realize they are expected to give. As a leader, you must make giving expectations clear *before* you invite someone to the board.

TAKEAWAY

- Do you model generous and sacrificial giving to your own organization?
- Have you personally experienced the joy of giving?
- Do you expect board members and your staff to give generously to your organization?
- Do you expect board members to raise funds for the organization in addition to giving? Do they know how?

What I do:

To encourage my staff, especially newcomers, to support the work, I invite field staff workers to give reports at team meetings. The staff are drawn toward workers who give touching reports, and it is natural to encourage them to support those individuals or at least join their newsletter lists.

6

Every Leader's Vulnerability

CHRISTIAN LEADERS UNWITTINGLY FALL INTO TWO extreme temptations when it comes to handling money. The first is a raw desire to have money—wanting to be rich. When Christian leaders embezzle money, the news media howls, but we cannot imagine those headlines could ever be about us.

The second is a desire *not* to have money—extreme asceticism.

We Christian leaders are vulnerable on both counts! When finances are tight, leaders are tempted to make questionable financial decisions they would never consider if they had full funding. Author Chris Wright warns: "Wherever there is money, there is temptation."[3]

The issue is not money itself but the *love of money*. Paul mentions it in his qualifications for leaders.

> *An overseer, then, must be...gentle, peaceable, **free from the love of money.** (1 Timothy 3:2–3, emphasis mine)*

Notice he doesn't say, "free from money." Managing money is necessary. The danger is getting hooked on money.

> *For the **love of money** is a root of all sorts of evil, and some by longing for it have wandered away from the faith, and pierced themselves with many griefs. (1 Timothy 6:10, emphasis mine)*

Though we are quick to criticize secular people who worship the almighty dollar, Paul is addressing Christians. A nonbeliever has no faith from which to wander.

Notice they didn't *bolt* from the faith. They *wandered* inch by inch, compromise by compromise, and "pierced themselves with many griefs."

Is Paul (the former Pharisee) basing his warnings on personal experience? In Jesus' day the Pharisees "were lovers of money" (Luke 16:14).

PRINCIPLE:

Leaders must be above reproach in financial dealings or they are disqualified for leadership.

Similarly, the apostle Peter warns leaders to shepherd the flock of God but "not for sordid gain" (1 Peter 5:2).

Years ago I was counseling a financially strapped Christian couple hooked on entering contests. They spent days filling out contest forms. Occasionally they won boxes of cereal, small cash, or dog food.

When her husband excused himself for a break, his wife described the day they were driving down Interstate 25 in Denver. Suddenly her husband pounded on the steering wheel with both hands and angrily shouted, "God, I wish I was rich!"

Oops. We wrongly assume only the rich want to be rich, but I find many rich people are not money hungry at all. In reality many poor people "long to be rich." Even Christian leaders can "long to be rich."

To determine how secure you are as a leader in regard to wealth, check how you act around wealthy people. Three reactions are common:

1. *Feel intimidated.* Coming from the Iowa farm I felt uncomfortable even talking with wealthy people. It starts with looking on the outward appearance and comparing ourselves with the wealthy. Then we feel powerless. But as Lauren Libby of Transworld Radio says, "Wealthy people put on their pants one leg at a time, just like we do."

2. *Hinting.* Finding themselves in the same room with wealth, some leaders use it as an opportunity to hint about their financial needs.

3. *Overly deferential.* When in the presence of wealth, some leaders become overly deferential or flattering. But flattery is for personal gain, not the other person's.

The second temptation I mentioned is more subtle — taking pride in asceticism. Some leaders believe poor funding is a mark of spiritual maturity, and they live in denial about the necessity of finances. Fearful of falling in love with "filthy lucre" (King James Bible), they excuse themselves from fundraising. They wrongly assume that being active in fundraising means they love money.

When leaders are poorly funded, what happens internally? Here's my story.

After college, Alma and I moved to Missouri with zero in the bank. Finally, I got a job, but my first paycheck was ten days away, and we had no food. So we collected pop bottles and redeemed them at the grocery store for nickels and dimes. With the coins, we bought yeast and Alma made bread. With that and a neighbor's tomato plant we didn't die. The "good old days!"

My mind was constantly churning about money, "Where is the next meal going to come from? How will I feed these kids?" Then guilt hit me. "I shouldn't worry. I must trust God." Back and forth the battle raged.

I wasn't thinking about my ministry assignment. I was thinking of *survival* interspersed by arguments with the devil. Good old days, indeed.

A few years ago a poorly funded missionary criticized me as we met for breakfast. He said, "I don't stoop to *asking*, like you do, Scott. I prefer to trust God." I kept quiet. He just stared at his pancakes. Then, in a broken voice, he admitted, "I think about money all the time."

When your staff are underfunded, they can't help but think about money all the time. In their resignation letters they claim they are quitting for "doctrinal differences," but money issues almost always lurk in the background.

TAKEAWAY

- Do you find yourself constantly wondering, "Where is the money going to come from?"

- Do you secretly believe that poor funding is more spiritual than full funding?

- Discuss with your staff: How do you act around rich people? What are your temptations with them?

- Discuss with your staff Chris Wright's statement, "Wherever there is money, there is temptation." Agree? Disagree?

What I do:

I love studying money passages with my staff, often as a devotional to start our meetings. For example, I say: Jesus warned in Luke 12:15 to be on guard against "every form of greed." The word used for greed (covetousness) is pleonexia (more—to have).

Perhaps you know the legendary millionaire John Rockefeller's response when asked how much money it took to be rich. "Just a little more."

Okay, how about you? What "forms of greed" tempt you—new cars, tech toys....what? I share first!

A Culture of Thankfulness Starts With You

RECENTLY MY WIFE ALMA AND I received an appeal from a mid-career friend who was joining a ministry. We gladly agreed to support her monthly and sent our first gift, then a second and a third. But neither our friend nor her organization acknowledged our giving. Were our gifts lost? After six months, the organization's leader sent an email gift-acknowledgement with an apology.

Hmmm. Not impressed.

Why are some mission workers and organizations slow to say thank you? Where did they get the idea that donors need nothing more than an occasional Mail Chimp update? I strongly suspect many have a sense of entitlement — Missionary Elitism: "I am called to ministry. I need not say thank you because I sacrifice so much for God."

Perhaps your culture doesn't put a high value on saying thank you *in writing*. Okay, then what is your plan to genuinely thank giving partners *soon* after they have given?

As a leader, do you model thankfulness to donors for your team? Some mission workers *intend* to consistently thank their giving partners but cannot find the time. I understand. I've been there. But the cycle of busyness must be broken. There is time in the work week to say thank you well.

Jesus valued thankfulness. He healed 10 lepers, but only one, a Samaritan (not a Jew!) came back to give honor and thanks to God. Jesus asked, "What about the nine?" Too busy?

How do we learn gratitude? I believe gratitude is learned from parents. As kids, if my brothers and I failed to thank our host after a nice meal, my mother marched us back into their home to say, "Thank you, Mrs. Jones. The dinner was delicious." Mechanical? Yes. But a lifelong habit was formed.

Today if you don't thank a grocery clerk who went to the back to get you fresh bananas, neither will you thank donors. Unfortunately, I have seen *godly* leaders display dismissive attitudes toward service industry workers — especially toward waiters at restaurants. Why is that? Entitlement?

PRINCIPLE:

Biblical leaders model expressing gratefulness to giving partners in timely and creative ways. Being careless in thanking donors reflects a weak understanding of God's grace.

A thankless attitude is serious! In Romans 1 Paul famously outlines the decline of civilization into debauchery with phrases like "they became futile in their speculations" and "worshipped and served the creature rather than the creator." But he adds, *"neither were they thankful."* Paul ranks thanklessness with other major sins!

As a leader you *must* model a culture of thankfulness. Perhaps thankfulness wells up inside you when you hear of a donor's gift, but does it translate into action? Your action or inaction in thankfulness will be copied by your staff.

Donna Wilson, Senior Consultant and National MPD Coach with Intervarsity wisely says, "Thanking needs to include information about the impact of the gift." I agree. Even a sentence or two helps donors feel they are an important part of your team. The few seconds of extra effort will be noticed.

Let us search our hearts to understand why gratitude is not our immediate response to giving partners.

TAKEAWAY

- Do you personally consider thanklessness a sin?

- Discuss thankfulness with your staff. Seek ways to creatively say thank you to giving partners, such as:

  - When a giving partner comes to mind in your devotions, text him: "Thought of you this morning. Thank you for being a partner and a friend."

  - Text two major donors from the airport. "Leaving for Dubai in a few minutes. Please pray for my presentations on servanthood. Appreciate you."

  - Upon your return from Dubai, send an email or social media thank you—three paragraphs with a photo of you in action. No attachments. No appeal.

  - When you travel, add a day to your itinerary to "enjoy their [donors] company for a while" (Romans 15:24).

  - Discuss: When you get a new giving partner, what memorable action can you take to welcome them to your funding team within 48 hours of discovering the gift?

  - With your staff, meditate on Romans 1 and Luke 17:15–16 looking for the theme of thanklessness.

What I do:

- At staff meetings I sometimes announce a do-it-now "Thankfulness Assignment" to write a short thank you to a donor. I supply stationery and postage. My assistant collects the letters and mails them immediately.

- I have a new donor welcome letter in my computer ready to send. I or my assistant merge the name and gift amount and mail it within a couple days with a small booklet as a "welcome to the team" gift.

Are You Convinced Giving is a Privilege?

IF YOU ARE NOT DEEPLY CONVINCED giving is a privilege, your success in fundraising will be stymied. You will:

- Waffle nervously at 'ask time'

- Find excuses to avoid fundraising

- Wallow in false guilt that you are taking money out of donors' pockets and putting it into yours

- Appeal only to those whom you think can afford it

So *is* giving a privilege? Perhaps you grew up with the view that giving is like paying a bill to God — something you *have to do* or God will be displeased. Similarly, in some cultures, tithing to the local church has become a legalistic burden. But what does the Bible say?

In Luke 21:1-4 the poor widow put two copper coins into the urn at the temple — "all she had to live on." Jesus "saw" her giving and even though she was poor, He did not stop her. Had it been me, I would have rushed in to say, "Wait a minute! You can't afford to give!"

But Jesus didn't stop her. Perhaps He was thinking of Deuteronomy 16:17 (NIV — emphasis mine):

> ***Each of you*** *must bring a gift in proportion to the way the Lord your God has blessed you.*

Each of you, according to what you received from the Lord. That includes the widow in Luke 21. I strongly believe that giving provides dignity, especially for the poor. It may be one of the only things a poor person can control.

My friend, John Gilberts of Greater Europe Mission, told me that their department used to go to downtown Colorado Springs monthly to pass out food and care packages for homeless people. Each staff member had five packets to give away, but John was having a great conversation about the gospel with one of the homeless and lost track of time. When he was supposed to leave, he still had another packet to pass out. Hesitatingly, he gave the packet to his new friend and asked him to give it to another homeless man.

PRINCIPLE:

Wise leaders strongly believe that biblical giving is not a burden but a privilege.

In his mind John thought, "He will likely keep the food for himself."

The next month when the team went downtown, John's homeless friend came running up to him. "I did it!" he exclaimed, "I gave it away." John's new friend thanked him for the privilege of giving.

Giving! A voluntary decision to give brings dignity and meaning to the giver — like the widow in Luke 21 and a homeless man in Colorado.

The Apostle Paul explains the personal blessing of giving. You know 2 Corinthians 9:7 where he says, "God loves a cheerful giver." But don't overlook the next verse:

> *And God is able to make all grace abound to you, so that always having all sufficiency in everything, you may have an abundance for every good deed... (2 Corinthians 9:8)*

Don't you want your giving partners to experience 'all grace abounding to them' and to have 'all sufficiency in everything?' This is not a promise of financial payback. "All grace" implies more than financial return. Why deny this 'promise' to anyone? When you focus on what donors have left after they give, you are looking at giving as a mere horizontal worldly transaction.

Note the last phrase, "have an abundance for every good deed." This implies they will receive even more, not to keep for themselves, but to continue giving. Good deeds cost money!

In 2 Corinthians 8:5 Paul says the Macedonians (new believers from Northern Greece) were "begging us for the favor of participation in support of the saints." What a refreshing view! If the Macedonians were in your church they would stand up and cheer when the offering basket was passed.

As a leader you do not have the right to *demand* that people give (1 Corinthians 9:12), but neither should you *deny* them the honor. Jesus didn't deny the widow the honor of giving. Let the donor decide.

Final thought: Since God is a joyful giver, doesn't it make sense that His creatures would be joyful givers too? If people criticize you for inviting them to give, perhaps they have not discovered the joy of giving.

TAKEAWAY

- What holds you back from boldness in fundraising? Is it because you wonder if God truly blesses the giver?
- Have you personally experienced the blessing of biblical generosity?
- If married, how does your spouse feel about biblical generosity? Talk it over.
- Discuss Luke 21:1–4 with your staff. Are they convinced giving is a privilege?
- Download "Appendix B: Creating Your Personal Giving Plan" to discuss with your staff and for your own study.

What I do:

On my Skype coaching calls with mission leaders I love sharing Luke 21:1–4. And they love talking about it because they have never seriously looked at this giving passage.

> And He looked up and saw the rich putting their gifts into the treasury. And He saw a poor widow putting in two small copper coins. And He said, "Truly I say to you, this poor widow put in more than all of them; for they all out of their surplus put into the offering; but she out of her poverty put in all that she had to live on."

I start by asking: "How much should a Christian give?" Usually the answer is "tithe." Then I challenge them to look at verse 4, which says she gave not ten percent but "all she had to live on." Did this widow give away all her assets? Was she irresponsible? The marginal reference says she gave "of the living that she had."

How much should a Christian give? I suggest: Give in such a way that it impacts your lifestyle (like the widow and unlike the rich in Luke 21).

Then we discuss the question: If your giving does not impact your lifestyle is it truly biblical giving?

You can have wonderful discussions with your staff on this passage. Dive in and see what happens.

Asking—Looking at Your Shoes

A GENEROUS FRIEND IN MINNEAPOLIS FREQUENTLY receives fundraising appeals from mission workers. "They come sheepishly to my office to ask for support for their work in Brazil or Germany or downtown," he told me, "but they have their heads down. Without looking me in the eye, they apologetically ask for funding. But I surprise them. 'Get your head up!' I bark. 'Stop looking at your shoes!'"

Did Moses have his head down when he invited the Jews to give toward the sanctuary — *begging* on behalf of a glorious God with whom he had just spent 40 glorious days? Can you imagine Moses saying to God, "You didn't tell me I'd have to beg."

As you think of your staff, do they realize that inviting God's people to participate in God's ministry is not *begging*? It's spiritual ministry — vertical, not horizontal. I find that even veteran workers are not immune to the *begging shadow* hanging over their fundraising. Help them sort it out.

In Philippians 4:18 Paul describes the Philippians' gift as a "fragrant aroma, well-pleasing to God." This word picture reminds us of the ancient Jews offering lambs on the altar with smoke ascending to heaven — vertically.

When your team understands that giving and receiving are vertical, begging need not be an issue. The late Catholic writer Henri Nouwen raises fundraising out of the begging morass:

> *"As a form of ministry, fundraising is as spiritual as giving a sermon, entering a time of prayer, visiting the sick or feeding the hungry."*[4]

Unfortunately, your staff's *feelings* about fundraising often overrule their intentions. They have excuses:

- I don't feel comfortable asking. It feels like begging.

- Our donors don't have much. They're poor.

- Asking will damage my friendships.

PRINCIPLE:

Biblical leaders are not neutral on fundraising. They take responsibility to see that their staff do not engage in apologetic fundraising.

They might not make overt excuses, but fundraising avoidance leaks out when they:

- Complain about having to do fundraising.

- Cut their budget to avoid having to raise so much.

- Find other *important* things to do rather than fundraising.

Do you hear these excuses from your team? If so, they are listening to culturally induced emotions rather than to God.

Don't let your staff dodge their leadership responsibilities merely because fundraising doesn't appeal to them. Furthermore, as their leader, you must not be *neutral* on fundraising. Being neutral immobilizes your staff. However, being bold in fundraising attracts other bold leaders and enables you to seize opportunities.

Maybe you are reacting to sleazy fundraising you see on late night television. Fine, reject that type of fundraising. Don't associate biblical fundraising with slick-haired hucksters — *double glazers* — as they are called in the United Kingdom.

Challenge your team to get their heads up and stop looking at their shoes! They are not beggars. They are like Moses coming off Mt. Sinai with a message from God and an invitation to friends to build God's Kingdom *together*!

TAKEAWAY

- To deepen your convictions about boldness meditate on these five Bible passages, one per day. Don't press for application. Let God's Spirit speak through His word.
  - Luke 8:1–3
  - Philippians 4:10–20
  - Romans 15:20–24
  - Nehemiah 1–2:8
  - 2 Corinthians 8–9

For an in-depth study of what the Bible says about fundraising, check out my book *Funding Your Ministry* at NavPress.com. In it I share how God freed me from the destructive belief that fundraising was begging.

- Do any of your staff have their heads down "looking at their shoes?" Of what are they embarrassed or ashamed?
- Do you have your head down?
- Discuss this chapter with your team and review the passages above.

What helps me:

We usually "look at our shoes" when we are with people we consider above us economically or socially. This reveals a latent fear of man, and it shows our eyes are on ourselves, not on God or the person we are asking. At such a time I quote Psalm 56:3–4:

> *When I am afraid [not if] I will put my trust in You...*
> *...I shall not be afraid. What can mere man do to me?*

It is okay to be afraid. It is not okay to live by fear of man. I also ask myself, "What is the worst that could happen?"

Your Team: Blind Spots As You Lead Others

Whether you are responsible for two staff or 15 or 150 or 1,500, you can unwittingly discourage them in fundraising in the words you say or don't say and in the actions you take or don't take. Most leaders have not been formally trained in how to develop a culture of biblical fundraising among their teams. And sadly, if your staff struggle in funding, you may not know—unless you talk to their spouses.

It's Their Problem, Right?

AS A FIELD SUPERVISOR YOU DID the right thing to send your staff for fundraising training. Now you can breathe a sigh of relief that their funding challenge is over!

But it is *not* over. Your staff must now put into practice what they learned, and a huge factor in their success is you — their supervisor! Even studies in the secular world show that the one-up supervisor is the key to employee job satisfaction. Please don't underestimate the role you play.

A study by the Stewardship Foundation of the United Kingdom found that UK mission workers self-reported their "biggest worry in ministry" is money. This was the main thing that "kept them awake at night." Work pressure was a distant second.[5]

Remember this as you lead your team — money is on their minds!

Let's start with a question that changes the paradigm: Y*our staff's funding — their problem, or yours?*

Just yesterday I heard about a gifted young campus staff person struggling with funding. His experienced, successful supervisor told him:

1. Reduce your budget; live on less.

2. Find a part-time job.

Outrageous! This leader was unwilling to *own* his staff member's financial challenge!

Because of the individualized nature of raising support, you might assume you don't need to help them — until they don't have money to travel to your quarterly meeting, or you get a tearful phone call from a spouse!

So how do you *lead* your staff to full funding? Bark at them to "get up to budget?" How about, "Work harder! But don't let your other responsibilities slip!" No! You can do better.

PRINCIPLE:

Because fundraising is part of ministry and included in staff job descriptions, leaders must take responsibility to share in their staff's funding challenges.

Here are a few action ideas:

A. Talk about fundraising unashamedly at every meeting.

But no poor talk! Complaining about the economy or joking about how *poor* you are dishonors the Lord and gives your staff permission to do the same. Create a *shame-free fundraising zone!* Try this:

- Each staff reports on a recent funding appointment. Celebrate successes and share difficulties.

- Study a scripture together such as Luke 8:1–3.

- Record names of the next five appointments, then pray.

- Discuss a provocative question such as, "Was Jesus poor or rich?" Use scripture.

- Share *your* most recent funding encounter — good or bad. Be vulnerable.

- List obstacles to full funding. Want the truth? Ask the spouses!

B. Go on funding appointments with your staff.

You will learn tons when you see them in action. And you will bond more deeply than merely drinking coffee together.

C. Find and develop a fundraising guru.

In any group of mission workers usually one has a knack for fundraising. Send her to training seminars and help her find resources (such as scottmorton.net). Give her a platform to teach at your meetings. Your guru should not be merely an *instinctive fundraiser,* unable to explain *how* she does it. In baseball, it is not the star players who become coaches.

D. Monitor each staff's fundraising report.

Without metrics you are stuck with anecdotal information such as "Our funding is good. God is faithful." That's a conversation stopper!

Also, don't be misled by the "percentage of budget" received. A staff worker proudly told me, "I am at 99 percent of budget." But that percentage was meaningless because he lowered his budget, and his wife (unwillingly but loyally) went back to work.

Metrics are the truth serum of fundraising! Before you meet with your staff member have him fill out "Appendix C: Up Till Now Report". From this data you can easily ask great questions and lay out action steps.

E. Establish a 100 percent policy.

Prohibit your staff from ministry until they are fully funded. Their spouses will thank you. You are not "being mean."

F. Fund their efforts.

It costs money to raise money. Pay for your staff's restaurant appointments or their travel to funding appointments during a thirty day window. First secure their action plans and their list of prospective donors.

G. Do it together.

On Your Own Fundraising (OYOF) is lonely! In Mombasa, Kenya,

Timm Njuguna and his wife Carol spent Thursday mornings with their staff studying funding passages, praying and phoning for appointments.

In Chicago, gospel workers did MNF — not Monday Night Football, but Monday Night Foning. The director provided pizza. Powerful.

Even if they cannot gather in one place, staff can Skype or Facetime with a partner. Recently two new staff let Skype run on mute while they both phoned, pausing to glance at each other now and then. Staff Trainer, Dave Dickens of Cru says, "Friends don't let friends phone alone."

H. Establish Funding Furloughs.

If your staff fall behind in funding, give them a 30–60 day funding furlough ministry assignment. Have them present a 30 day fundraising plan for approval by you or a funding guru. Officially agree that they will withdraw 50–90 percent from their normal ministry work. Monitor compliance because they want to 'sneak' back to their normal routines. Encourage your staff by helping fund their fundraising expenses.

I. Ask five key questions.

You may be so overwhelmed you cannot imagine tackling your staff's fundraising issues. You can still lead by asking five questions:

1. *Tell me about your fundraising. How are you **feeling**?* (Don't stop after this question!)

2. *How much per month are you trying to raise — what is your 'holy number' — the exact amount you need to be at full funding?* If she does not know her 'holy number' why not? This implies your organization has a standard budget allowance scale. Don't make your staff guesstimate their budget.

3. *Tell me about your last two funding appointments. What was the donor's response?*

4. *To spouse (if married): How do **you** feel about the fundraising? Do you accompany your spouse on funding appointments? What role can you play in the funding strategy?*

5. *What will it take for you to become fully funded in the next six months? How can our team help?* Connect him with your local funding guru.

In conclusion, the best thing a one-up leader can do is model, either in personal or corporate fundraising. If you lack confidence in fundraising, your words and body language have already given you away! But you can still lead. Admit your struggles and your staff's morale will soar.

TAKEAWAY

- Which two suggestions from A-B-C-D-E-F-G-H-I can you implement first?
- What can you cut out to give yourself time to serve your staff to reach full funding?

What I do:

I have learned to ask my staff (with spouse if married):

- What would it look like for you to take 30-days away from your regular ministry for a special fundraising assignment? (Don't accept a "two years from now" answer.)
- Let's figure out together the best 30-day time frame? (I offer to relieve them of other responsibilities as needed.)
- What can I do to help you recruit 30 new giving partners during these 30 days?

Ignoring Your Economic Engine?

IN MINISTRIES LIKE CRU, YWAM, INTERVARSITY, The Navigators, Wycliffe, and many others, field staff raise 80 to 90 percent of all gift income. But too often, leaders and boards focus on the 10–20 percent needed for corporate funding — capital campaigns, office funds and special projects. They neglect the economic driver — staff funding!

Because headquarters is silent, you as a field supervisor must champion your staff in funding, even when it seems non-urgent.

Your guiding star is Hezekiah, the 25 year old courageous King of Judah. When he became CEO in 725 B.C., the Levites (full-time workers of the Jewish culture) were poorly funded.

His predecessor, King Ahaz, "closed the doors of the house of the Lord and made altars for himself in every corner of Jerusalem" (2 Chronicles 28:24). King Ahaz worshipped the gods of Aram and even practiced child sacrifice.

To bring the nation back to God, surprisingly Hezekiah launched a fundraising campaign for the Levites — his full-time workers.

> *"Also he commanded the people who lived in Jerusalem to give the portion due to the priests and the Levites, [tithe — ten percent] that they [the Levites] might devote themselves to the law of the LORD."* (2 Chronicles 31:4)

Also surprisingly, the people gave so generously they piled the tithed grain in heaps on the streets — a successful campaign.

I realize you contend daily with wildly burning grass fires and don't feel you have capacity (like Hezekiah) to champion your staff in funding. The higher up the organization you go, the more removed this problem becomes. It is assumed field staff eventually figure out how to get their funding. A gifted few survive, but most do not.

They:

- Quit soon after orientation.

- Cut back to part time.

- Lower their budget.

- Encourage their spouse to work outside the ministry.

PRINCIPLE:

Leaders, Boards and CEO's must champion the funding of their field staff—the organizational economic engine.

Hezekiah took Levite funding seriously and so must you. More pragmatically, if your office is funded by a percentage charge on field staff income, then the economics alone should get your attention.

Notice I am saying *champion* your support raising staff. You do not have to be the expert to coach each one.

Unlike Hezekiah, you can't *command* donors to support your field staff, but you can use these questions to determine if you as a leader are doing all you can to help your staff reach full funding:

- *Do your staff receive excellent fundraising training?*

  If it's merely a few hours of talking-head orientation, it's not *excellent*!

- *Do you provide your staff with quality fundraising materials? Do they use them?*

  Your organizational brochure or website is not focused enough for fundraising. If you expect staff to create their own materials be prepared for embarrassment!

- *Does each new staff have a fundraising coach?*

  Coaches could be experienced field staff or Development or HR staff, but not their immediate supervisor. Supervisors too often naively allow staff to launch ministry before they are fully funded, usually with dire consequences years later.

- *Do you hold your staff accountable in funding?*

Do both coach and supervisor receive reports on funding progress, especially of new staff? Don't let "happy talk" snooker you. Trust but verify! Does your organization have an easy to use fundraising progress report for staff to send to their coach and supervisor? You are welcome to customize "Appendix C: Up Till Now Report".

- *Are you modeling in fundraising?*

Modeling beats pep talks!

- *Do you have an organizational policy on full funding? Is it enforced?*

Do not allow your staff to go into ministry partially funded. Without a full-funding policy no amount of training will suffice.

- *Do you provide seed money?*

It takes money to raise money. In Kenya, former mission director, Stanley Mukolwe, bought cell phone airtime for his staff at funding seminars. Upon receiving airtime, one Kenyan exclaimed, "My phone has never had so many minutes! I thought it was going to explode!" He knew his leader cared about him.

- *Do you publicly commend your gift income staff?*

"On behalf of the entire ministry, thank you for your hard work in fundraising."

If field staff are not championed in fundraising, everyone loses. Staff dreams are dashed. The organization has fewer workers with time to focus on the mission. Headquarters receives lower field charge income. But most importantly, the oppressed people whom you want to touch remain without hope. All because leadership neglected the economic engine in funding.

CEO's and national leaders: Here is another reason to champion field staff. Even if every staff on your team is at 100 percent of budget, you will still not have enough money! Sooner or later, you will need expansion funds — unless you are not planning to expand!

Donor gifts to an individual field staff top out at $5,000 to $10,000 annually. The amount varies outside the US. One giving partner told me, "I will not give more than $500 per month ($6,000 per year) to your support. I do not want you to become overly dependent on me!"

Major donors cap their gifts for staff, but they have more to give. Invite them to give (in addition to their staff support) for national or regional projects — the ones that sit on your desk unfunded right now.

Field staff may resent you soliciting "their donors." In my former role as Director of Development I know of no cases where a donor dropped a field staff to support national projects. Also, the more projects or staff a partner supports the more likely he or she will give for a long time.

Instead of arguing with field staff about "who owns the donor" (legally, the organization does and spiritually God does) offer this: "For every donor you lose because of a corporate funding appeal from my office, I will give you double what that donor has given you in the past year." (You won't have to pay a shilling or a kwacha or a peso.)

To summarize: Though it may seem non-urgent, invest heavily in the economic engines of your organization — your gift income field staff!

Former U.S. President Dwight Eisenhower famously said: "What is important is seldom urgent, and what is urgent is seldom important." Like young Hezekiah, champion your gift income staff! It is important, and it is urgent!

Lauren Libby, President of TransWorld Radio, says it best: "If field staff ain't happy, nobody's happy!"

TAKEAWAY

- Do your gift income staff:
  - Receive excellent fundraising training?
  - Receive fundraising materials they are proud of?
  - Have skilled coaches holding them accountable in funding?
  - Adhere to your full-funding organizational policy?
- Are you deliberately identifying and recruiting your staff's 'major do-nors' for corporate support?
- What is one action step you are ready to implement from the bullet list above?

Casting Vision is Not Enough

VISION—"PAINTING AN INSPIRING PREFERRED future" is what leaders do, but vision casting alone will not get you to where you want to go. And though they won't tell you, your team is demoralized by your visionary pep talks when they are not up to budget.

What must you add to your vision? *Timber.*

Many leadership sermons have been preached about Nehemiah rebuilding Jerusalem's walls in only 52 days while under Persian occupation in 450 B.C. How did Nehemiah motivate these discouraged Jews to "arise and build" amidst withering opposition?

You've read Nehemiah's story. He was in exile serving the King of Persia 700 miles across the desert from his beloved Jerusalem. An entourage came from Jerusalem and reported the sad state of the city with its broken down walls, allowing enemies to freely enter.

Nehemiah was heartbroken and driven to prayer. During his six months in prayer and sadness he formulated a plan, *and a funding tactic.* He approached King Artaxerxes in Nehemiah 2:7-8:

> *And I said to the king, "If it please the king, let letters be given me for the governors of the provinces beyond the River, that they may allow me to pass through until I come to Judah, and a letter to Asaph the keeper of the king's forest, that he may give me timber to make beams for the gates of the fortress which is by the temple...*

Though he was a big thinking vision caster, a passionate prayer warrior, and a detailed planner, those strengths were *not* the key to his success. Nehemiah succeeded because he brought *timber* from the king's forest. Resources!

Imagine if Nehemiah had shown up in Jerusalem without timber. Perhaps the conversation with the beaten down Jews would have gone like this:

PRINCIPLE:

Vision without resources to accomplish the vision is merely visionary. Leaders bring resources to the task.

Nehemiah: "Listen people! God has given me a grand vision to rebuild the city walls and gates. Let's trust God together! We can do it!"

Jerusalem Elders: "Rebuild? How?"

Nehemiah: "God has spoken to me! If we just work together and pray and sacrifice and..."

Jerusalem Elders: "Fine, but what do we build with? We have no timber for gates or scaffolding! The few trees around Jerusalem are scraggly, burned for fuel long ago."

Here is Nehemiah's secret: Leaders bring resources to the task. Or as my friend Okike Offia from Nigeria says, "Vision without funding is a mirage."

Your followers need more than vision pep talks! If they don't have resources they cannot execute.

What does "timber" look like? It could be emergency cash to a beleaguered field rep, a new computer for an overstretched assistant, reference books for a young scholar or a plane ticket for a staff intern.

Here is a classic story about providing timber.

Missions pioneer and Pearl Harbor survivor Jim Downing was visiting a collegiate summer training fraternity in the Midwest. At 7:30 a.m. a student trainee was struggling to jumpstart his car to make it to his new job across town. His team leader was helping him in the parking lot, but it wasn't going well. Quickly the young student lost patience and began shouting. His anger raged out of control.

Jim was watching from an upper story window. Finally, the car roared to a start and in a cloud of gravel, the angry student sped off, late for work. Later, the team leader told Jim how frustrating that parking lot experience had been and asked Jim for suggestions about how to help the student when he returned home at 5 p.m.

"Shall I talk to him about anger? Or perhaps do a Bible study on trusting God?" the team leader asked.

Wisely, Jim replied, "Why don't you buy him a new battery?"

That's timber!

Here's another example:

A young city minister was struggling in his fundraising and called me for advice. I suggested he take two weeks to focus on funding. He perked up as I helped him identify 15 potential donors who needed to hear his story.

Then silence. The phone went cold. Problem?

Finally, it came out. He lived in Baltimore, but his prospective donors were in Atlanta. He couldn't afford his fundraising. By God's grace (and with office funds set aside for helping staff), I offered to pay for an airplane ticket and rental car if he could stay with friends in Atlanta. Done!

*Two weeks later he joyfully reported a handful of new monthly donors. My "leadership" would have been worthless if I had not provided **timber**!*

Save your pep talk breath to cool your coffee! Saying to your staff, "I'll pray for you!" but taking no action is bad leadership. Give your staff the resources they need to get their jobs done and watch productivity and morale soar!

What about stipends? **Timber** is not the same as a stipend. I have found stipends (automatic payments or salary boosts) do not work for the long term. Organizations paying stipends for specified months or years risk trouble. When the stipend period finishes, the staff quits. Not always, but frequently.

Timber supplies a needed item that maximizes the staff's work here and now. It is not a subsidy but meets a need they cannot supply for themselves. If you use stipends for intern staff (for example) make sure part of their job during their internship is building their donor base for the long term.

TAKEAWAY

- Evaluate your words to your staff. Is it mostly visionary happy talk? Do you ask them what they need to get the job done?

- Who on your staff needs timber right now? Do you have funds to help them?

Team member: *What kind of timber do they need?*

1. _____ _____

2. _____ _____

3. _____ _____

4. _____ _____

Question:

Is it possible to help too much? Will I 'enable' my staff to become over-ly dependent on me?

Answer:

Yes. Too much help backfires. Don't do for them what they can do for themselves. And if you worry more about the outcome than they do, helping will only hurt. Find out why they care so little about their funding.

Is God Involved in Your Fundraising?

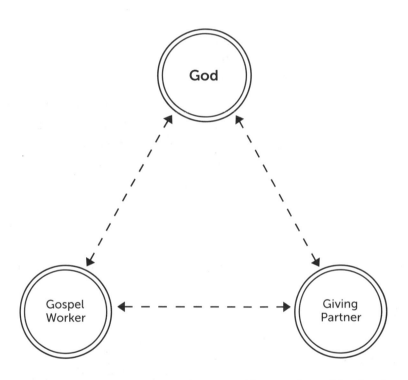

IN HIS EXCELLENT BOOK, THE GOD ASK, my colleague Steve Shadrach says three parties are involved in fundraising — the worker (asker), the partner (giver) and the Lord — as in his triangle diagram adapted from his book.

This is why I do not ask, "Will you give?" But rather, "Will you *pray* about joining our team with a gift of _____ each month?" I want giving partners to seek the Lord for how *He* wants them to handle *His* money. This reminds your partners that they are managing Somebody else's stuff!

Not only do we want our giving partners to pray before they decide on giving, we also must bring prayer into the entire fundraising process.

PRINCIPLE:

Biblical fundraising is more than a mere horizontal transaction. Since both giver and asker are stewards, not owners, God must be involved in both the giving decision and the appeal process.

As a leader, you pray before making decisions, right? You ask for God's wisdom before finalizing the site of your staff conference — New Orleans or New York. And you breathe a prayer as you share Christ with a neighbor. Is it only in fundraising that we skip praying?

Nehemiah didn't skip praying. When his friends came to Persia bringing the discouraging report that the wall of Jerusalem was damaged and the people were in pain, he did not take immediate action. Instead, he first went to prayer.

You can easily spot his heartfelt intercessory prayer for Jerusalem in Nehemiah 1:5–10. Besides intercession, he demonstrates two other prayer disciplines. Both are important as you lead your team in funding.

The first is *confession.*

> *We have acted very corruptly against You and have not kept the commandments… (Nehemiah 1:7)*

Confession unmasks our below the surface selfish desires. After confessing our sins, we are humbled and find ourselves thinking more like God thinks. Confession helps us see we are part of *His* vision more than Him being part of ours.

Secondly, Nehemiah reminds God of His ancient promise to bring back the Jews from Persia — he was *"claiming a promise."*

> [8] *"Remember the word which You commanded Your servant Moses, saying, 'If you are unfaithful I will scatter you among the peo-*

ples; ⁹ but if you return to Me and keep My commandments and do them, though those of you who have been scattered were in the most remote part of the heavens, I will gather them from there and will bring them to the place where I have chosen to cause My name to dwell.(Nehemiah 1:8, 9)

Yet I struggle in praying. I want to claim promises, but I have the attention span of a teenage grasshopper hopped up on an energy drink. My praying is interspersed with daydreaming about my baseball days at Iowa State (should have thrown a curve!) So, to concentrate in prayer I have written three Bible promises in my journal, and I pray through these promises nearly every day:

John 15:16 promises a Christ follower that if we "go and bear fruit" that "our fruit will remain." I want my work to 'remain' — not to come unstuck in two days or two years.

Isaiah 58:10–12 promises that if I "give myself to the hungry" that I will be like a "watered garden," and "those from among you will rebuild the ancient ruins." It will not be me who rebuilds the ancient ruins but those to whom I have poured out my life.

Psalm 126:6 says, "He who goes to and fro weeping, carrying his bag of seed shall indeed come again with a shout of joy, bringing his sheaves with him." God impressed me for years to keep on sharing the gospel, and He will ensure that it will result in sheaves of grain. Not by my power but His.

Not only do we claim promises, but as International Missions Statesman, Mike Treneer, reminds us, "Let His promises claim *you*." God is fulfilling His design. Remind yourself that you are part of it.

Back to Nehemiah. After five months of mourning and praying, his opportunity came to appeal to King Artaxerxes, but he was "very much afraid" (Nehemiah 2:2).

Artaxerxes noticed Nehemiah's sad countenance and asked, "What would you request?" Because praying was interwoven into his life, Nehemiah offered a spontaneous prayer "to the God of heaven" (2:4). Then he presented a well thought out plan with an appeal.

Nehemiah's praying shows his appeal was not merely horizontal. It included himself, Artaxerxes, and the Lord, like *The God Ask* diagram above.

Where to start? Pray daily for your funding goals to be 100 percent met— both your personal ministry budget and your city, regional or national budget. "Give us this day our daily bread" (Matthew 6:11). Your "daily bread" is your budget.

In my daily prayer journal I record my exact ministry budget and the names of potential donors, including a specific amount I intend to invite each one to pray about giving. When I phone to arrange a meeting, the person for whom I have been praying often says, "Scott, it is amazing you called today. We were just talking about you last night!" Coincidence?

I once listed $100 monthly beside the names of four friends — fearfully.

Within a few months, three started at $100 per month. But I heard nothing from the fourth — "75% is not bad," I congratulated the Lord. But on December 31 the fourth gift appeared in my account — $1,200, an average of $100 per month! Four of four! Thanks to the Lord.

Today in addition to my personal support *holy number*, I also ask God to bring in the exact budget of my team, the International Office.

Sadly, mission leaders today sometimes do not even know their budgets. How can they pray for it? Take time to "know well the state of your flocks" (Proverbs 27:23).

Is the triangle diagram too simple? Absolutely not! Without bringing God into our fundraising we are counting on self-effort.

What about your staff? How can you help them bring God into their fundraising? Rob Mahon, Albuquerque City Director, does something that is reproducible for us all. Once a month he hosts a funding breakfast where one by one each staff member answers:

- What have you done in fundraising since our last breakfast?

- What is your 'holy number' (new funding needed)?

- What will you do in fundraising before the next breakfast?

Then they pray together specifically for one another's holy number. No shame, no judgmental spirit. No other topics are on the agenda. At first the staff were timid to answer Rob's three questions, but now they love it. The monthly breakfast serves as a morale boost for the entire team.

TAKEAWAY

- Can you state your specific budget right now for your personal ministry? For your organization? For your staff members? Write it in your prayer journal!

- Are you asking for your 'daily bread,' your budgets, and for your potential donors with amounts? Daily!

- Learn your staff's individual funding challenges and their 'holy numbers'—the exact amounts they need to raise. That communicates powerfully that you care about them not only as 'staff' but as human beings.

- What do you need to confess as you move into fundraising?

- Do you have a special promise or two that God put in the Bible especially for you? How about sharing your promises with your team?

- Who are five potential giving partners you'd like to invite for support? What amount or range would you like each one to pray about?

Name of potential partner	Project	Amount to ask
1. _____	_____	$ _____
2. _____	_____	$ _____
3. _____	_____	$ _____
4. _____	_____	$ _____
5. _____	_____	$ _____

What I do:

When staff are overwhelmed by the immensity of their holy number, I simply pray with them, saying: "Our Father in Heaven, [Bob and Sally] are overwhelmed, but they are going to work hard on their funding plans. Father, they are counting on You—the Source of all. We pray together that You would miraculously appear as they phone for appointments and as they meet with partners—especially [J and S]. Would you prepare them to consider $5,000 annually..."

Your Staff Fear This Question

I HAVE YET TO MEET A ministry worker who has not been asked, "Why don't you get a real job?" We even remember where and when. For me, it was outside our home in Iowa, one cool October afternoon when my kindhearted mother asked, "Couldn't you go to seminary and be a pastor instead of a missionary?"

When your staff are ambushed by the *real job* question, doubts creep in about their legitimacy, especially if they work in a culture that doesn't esteem gift income workers outside the local church.

If your staff do not believe they are legitimate servants of the King, you will lose them, especially when their finances are weak. This question slithers in and out of their minds like a beady-eyed grass snake, unseen and ominous. Do not leave them alone to struggle.

Missionary legitimacy is not new. Paul dealt with it in Corinth. To help your staff understand their legitimacy, study 1 Corinthians 9 with them. A little background:

According to the *Dictionary of Paul and his Letters*, Greek philosophers charged fees for their teaching or were funded by wealthy patrons.

The Corinthians suspected Paul wasn't a bona fide apostle because he would not accept financial support. Besides that, the Corinthian church had problems; competitive spirit, sexual scandal, and eating meat offered to idols, to name three.

Because of Paul's example here, I do not invite gifts from extremely problem plagued individuals. Once I accepted a ministry gift from a mentally troubled young man and later got a nasty call from his mother. In retrospect, he was giving only to manipulate me. Warn your staff to be careful.

From this no win pot of soup Paul writes 1 Corinthians 9, the "rights chapter," a theological defense for the right of Kingdom workers to receive support from believers. He formulates the question in verses 1–6:

> *Do we not have a right to eat and to drink [at the expense of the churches]? (verse 4 Amplified Bible)*

Lawyer like, in verses 7–14 Paul presents the *Five L's* argument:

* Logic:

  "Who at any time serves as a soldier at his own expense...who tends a flock and does not use the milk of the flock" (verse 7)? So ministers may receive from their flocks.

* Law:

  "You shall not muzzle the ox while he is threshing" (verse 9 quoting Deuteronomy 25:4). Let the ox dip his head for a mouthful of grain as he treads the stalks. Paul said this verse was written for our sakes, not for oxen. Humorously Martin Luther said, "Can oxen read?"

* Loyalty to teachers:

  "If we sowed spiritual things in you, is it too much if we reap material things from you?" (verse 11). The receivers of the gospel are expected to share financially with their teachers. *Also Romans 15:27 "they are indebted to minister to them also in material things."*

* Levitical example:

  "...and those who attend regularly to the altar have their share from the altar," (verse 13). Paul has the Levites in mind.

* Lord Jesus:

  "So also the Lord directed those who proclaim the gospel to get their living from the gospel" (verse 14). Paul's ringing conclusion para-

phrases Jesus' instructions to the twelve disciples: *"The worker is worthy of his support."* (Matthew 10:10)

Paul makes Jesus' principle the capstone of his argument. Wow!

Be confident mission leader! Don't let the *real job* criticism define you or your staff. If you are called to advance the kingdom, you have the right to be supported by gifts. Listen to your Caller, not your culture.

If you have staff in their 20's and 30's they are especially vulnerable to the *real job* question. Teach them this passage right away — I mean right away! Help them deal with the dreaded question before it comes.

TAKEAWAY

- Which of your team members brood over the "real job" question? Do you?
- As a leader, what organizational legitimacy can you provide? Do your staff have:
  - Organizational brochures and fundraising tools?
  - Job descriptions?
  - Job reviews?
  - Official salary scale?
  - Organizational website?
  - Office location?
- Have you studied 1 Corinthians 9 with your staff?

ABFR Will Attack Your Team

ABFR — Anything But FundRaising.

AT A LIVELY SEMINAR WITH GOSPEL leaders in Burkina Faso, West Africa, I was explaining that full funding is only possible if they take time to do it, up to 20 percent of their week. Suddenly the talkative audience fell silent. This was new doctrine. Finally, from the back of the room a veteran Nigerian cautiously raised his hand.

"Yes, Zeke."

With a sigh Zeke said, "Twenty percent takes time away from my ministry. *Isn't there another way?*" Everyone nodded at Zeke and then turned to me.

Yes, there is *another way*. There are many ways! God funded His ministers through tithing, ravens, a widow, a pagan king, making tents, worthy hosts, Roman magistrates, direct appeals, generous women travelers, grateful parishioners, and third party appeals.

Why be stuck on one way if the Bible reveals many ways? Consider these alternatives to raising personal support:

- BAM — Business As Mission. Let business profits support you.

- Minister part time as a tentmaker.

- Fund yourself via investments or savings.

- Be seconded to a local church that guarantees your salary.

- Spouse works an outside job.

- Charge fees to companies for your coaching services.

- Join a centrally funded organization that pays a guaranteed salary.

If your staff are discouraged in funding, these alternatives will attract them like cool water to a Kenyan marathon runner. One young leader told me angrily, "I am called to ministry, not fundraising!"

Switching to an alternative method *feels* like the will of God because it reduces the pressure of fundraising. But are your staff being seduced by the ABFR Syndrome — *Anything But FundRaising*?

To combat the ABFR Syndrome you must help your team survive the emotions of fundraising and bring them back to objectivity. Discuss these four questions with them:

Question 1: Are there downsides to raising personal support?
Absolutely. Here are four:

- Raising support takes time, especially face to face appeals.

- The organization loses donors when "their missionary" leaves.

- Donors from cultures without a history of monthly support often give only one-off gifts or nothing.

- Staff from non-evangelical backgrounds struggle to create a large mailing list of potential donors.

Question 2: Is there a positive side to personal support?
Yes! Here are four.

- People give to people.

  A giving partner from Minneapolis died last year. "Richard and Judy" had supported us at a meager $25 per quarter. A few weeks after Richard's funeral, Judy phoned me. I volunteered, "Judy, I understand if you must stop support. Your income is lower now."

  "Absolutely not." she said. "I am going to cut two national organizations, but I am not going to stop supporting *our missionaries*."

  Our missionaries! People give to people. Those who have never lived on personal support do not understand the emotional bond between donors and *their* missionaries.

- *Expansion.* Decentralized fundraising by staff workers expands ministry more quickly than by centralized fundraising. Staff recruit donors who know them, whereas central fundraising depends on the skill of the home office. Also, centralized fundraising requires a costly home office fundraising department.

- *Blesses givers.* Jesus could have funded his ministry with business income as a carpenter, or he could have lived off savings. Instead, He chose to be supported by giving partners who had been touched by His work (Luke 8:1–3). With designated support, you bless others.

- *Growth for the worker.* In Matthew 10 Jesus could have given the disciples travel money as He sent them out (as did our baseball coach at Iowa State for weekend trips). Or He could have told them to fund their travel from their savings or to find a job at their destination. Instead, He instructed the disciples to find faithful 'worthy men' to host them.

  Two benefits emerged from Jesus' strategy. It blessed the generous "worthy hosts," and it enlarged the disciples' trust. I have found that fundraising forces me to deepen my trust in the Lord, confront my fears, stop being insecure, and become articulate — fast!

Question 3: Why do you want to switch to an alternative method of funding?

If you don't like fundraising, admit it. But identify *why* you don't like it — out of contacts, fear of rejection, pressure from family — there is a reason! But if you switch to a non-fundraising method, you will lose the "cloud of witnesses" who pray as well as give.

Question 4: Will business as mission (BAM) reduce fundraising pressure?

'BAM' is an important mission strategy with good potential to penetrate the culture, but what does it actually mean? Shouldn't every business run by believers be a *mission*?

Let's not be naïve. A missions pastor at a major church tells me that many of the 'business as mission' projects he investigates would fail dramatically if the leaders were not underwritten by the personal support of faithful donors. "To be honest," he said, "it is a business as mission/support hybrid."

He also said that most mission workers are "poor at running businesses, especially in foreign cultures." Many mission businesses fail. Nevertheless, business as mission is a good alternative in cultures that prohibit the gospel. John Gilberts, COO of Greater Europe Mission summarizes: "BAM should be primarily a ministry strategy, not a funding strategy, and it should be run by experienced business people."

BAM enables you to more easily answer the question, "What are you doing in my country?" But BAM does not reduce financial pressure. You now are trying to make a long term business succeed, and that is tough! According to the US Department of Labor in America, only 30 percent of new businesses endure beyond ten years, and that is not operating in cross-cultural settings.

My friend Irene, a gospel worker in Nigeria, started her own business, and she is succeeding. But listen to her sobering observation: "If you want to start a business so you will have more time for ministry and create better funding, be careful. You will not have as much time as you think, and you will not make as much money as you think." Wow.

Okay, let's draw a conclusion. How would the apostle Paul answer Zeke's question: "Is there another way?"

Paul ministered sometimes as a full-time gift income leader and sometimes as a conventional income tentmaking leader. His guideline: "I do all things for the sake of the gospel" (1 Corinthians 9:23).

Following Paul's guideline, objectively ask yourself: In my context, what method of funding best advances the gospel? Your *comfort* is not the issue. Your *preference* on fundraising is not the issue. The deciding factor is: What advances the gospel best? It is not about you.

Please do not be seduced by ABFR syndrome. If you don't like fundraising, admit it. Then identify exactly why. Perhaps you will discover a blindspot.

TAKEAWAY

- What is at the bottom of your staff's discomfort with fundraising? Lack of competence in fundraising? Lack of teamwork? Family pressure? Fear? Understand the emotions.

- Ask your staff: In your context, what type of fundraising advances the gospel the best?

- What do you risk by not raising support?

What Are You Asking For?
(That's What You'll Get!)

JOIN ME IN A CONVERSATION WITH an excited leader who had just scored some yeses to his funding appeals.

Scott: What did you ask the donors to do?

Excited Worker: I asked them to give, and they did!

Scott: Did you ask for ongoing support — monthly or annual?

Excited Worker (a little defensively): No. I'm just glad they gave! Maybe I was nervous, but I got their gifts! (triumphantly)

Scott: Did you ask for a specific amount?

Excited Worker: No, I'm just glad they gave!

How would you handle this? Do you see a problem here?

Staff who lack confidence in funding are too easily satisfied with one-off ("one-time") gifts and too easily satisfied with tiny amounts. If I could do my early ministry years over again, I would ask for bigger gifts (monthly and annual). Because I worried about offending potential donors, I "low-balled" my appeals.

Securing only one-off gifts or small gifts is like putting $1 worth of gas into a 15 gallon tank over and over and over.

Many gifts are one-off because staff do not *ask* for monthly or annual support. And many gifts are small because they *ask* small. That is "leaving money on the table" (as we say in America). You get what you ask for. Is your goal to simply 'find money' or recruit loyal ongoing giving partners?

In conducting fundraising training in 25 cultures around the world, I observe that most mission workers come across as too timid, and they ask too small.

PRINCIPLE:

Leaders work to develop faithful giving partners. They are not desperate merely to find money.

How about your staff? Are they "glad just to get a gift?" Teach them to think about the future and seek long-term partners, not simply one-off small gifts! Their giving partners should feel like they are joining a dynamite vision, not bailing out a charity.

Let's learn from Jesus Himself. His giving partners were not one-off donors. Though we don't know the size of their gifts, we do know that the women who supported Jesus early in his ministry in Galilee were still attending to Him at the crucifixion two years later. Not only that, some of them traveled 70 miles to Judea. More amazing is Acts 1:14 where Jesus' followers were huddled after the resurrection "along with the women." What women? The women from Luke 8:1–3 and Matthew 27:55–56 — the *donors* were continuing!

In the Scriptures we see examples of repeated giving:

- Joash told the Levites to "repair the house of your God *annually*" (emphasis mine). The temple needed ongoing maintenance (2 Chronicles 24:5).

- The Apostle Paul commended the Philippians for sending him "a gift more than once" (Phil 4:16).

Of course, not every giving partner wants to give monthly or annually. And not every partner can give larger gifts, but don't deny them the opportunity. Giving partners of all sizes are needed, and all are valued in God's eyes.

Can you offend people by asking for larger gifts? Not likely in face to face settings. I find that donors are flattered that I thought they could give that much. Of course, be wise. Do not ask a college student in your Bible study for $10,000 per year, and do not appeal to a wealthy business executive for $10 per month.

What about special "one-off" projects? Yes, special projects (for local or corporate support) should be part of your funding strategy once or twice a year — but not every time you run out of cash!

Note the date of your 'one-off' gifts. At the six month or 11 month anniversary of each gift ask the giver to "do it again." Even if a donor says he is giving a 'one-time-gift' that doesn't mean you can't come back for a 'one-time-gift' next year, especially if you have faithfully sent newsletters thanking him and explaining the impact of his giving.

Your special project givers are good candidates to invite as monthly or anchor donors.

TAKEAWAY

Here are some ideas to help your staff and organization promote ongoing support and increase gift size:

- Do your receipts have a "next gift" response device so donors can easily send another gift?

- Are your staff asking for ongoing monthly and annual support? How do you know?

- Are your staff asking for significant gifts? How do you know?

- Does your development team position their appeals with future gifts in mind? Or are you pressing them for this year's budget only?

- Do your staff know how to ask one-off or erratic donors at the eleven month anniversary of their last gift to "do it again?" Tons of support is lost here.

- Can donors sign up for electronic monthly bank draft giving or recurring credit card giving on your website without human intervention?

- Discuss with your staff: What is the largest gift you ever asked for? What happened?

What I did:

As I continued in leadership, I realized I would never be fully funded by smaller gifts and one-off gifts. So I worked with my budget (and my calendar) and found that if I had ten $100-$150 monthly partners and three $5,000-$10,000 per year partners I could be fully funded within a year.

I prayerfully identified 15 people on my mailing list and started phoning for appointments. With trepidation, I explained my plan face to face, one at a time to the 15, most of whom were already giving one-off or smaller amounts. They took my numbers seriously! I got what I asked for, but I didn't pick those amounts out of the air. I did my homework.

Three Fundraising Culs-de-sac

CUL-DE-SAC #1. YEARS AGO A WELL-KNOWN Evangelical conference and radio speaker lamented to me: "Our funding keeps going down even though I am speaking more and sending over 1,000 newsletters."

Cul-de-sac #2. I recently counseled with a start-up ministry that planned to spend a ton of money to "increase visibility" so they could raise money.

Cul-de-sac #3. Some mission leaders 'hint' about their funding. "People 'catch on,'" they say with a wink.

Behind these three examples lie three faulty assumptions:

- Money follows *information.*

- Money follows *visibility.*

- Money follows *hinting.*

As a leader, guard your staff from falling into these popular but ineffective funding culs-de-sac. Of course, information and visibility, like sending newsletters broadly to cultivate the interest of non-donors, are an important part of your funding strategy.

But few people give merely because they are *aware* of you or because you are *visible* to the public eye, or because they have received your hints. They do not go to bed at night burdened by your lack of support. They are wondering how many text messages they are accumulating or how to get their teenage daughter to a nunnery.

Even if potential donors have information about your work, even if you are highly visible, few will support you unless they are asked. And the most effective way to ask 99 percent of the time is face to face. The yes-rate for face-to-face appeals around the world with those trained in face-to-face appeals is 50–70 percent.

However, many leaders believe that asking is sub-spiritual. The *accidental* patron saint of the *no-ask model* is George Mueller of Bristol, England who "told only God." In the late 1800's abundant funding flowed to Mueller's orphanages year after year.

PRINCIPLE:

Money follows face to face asking.

But do your staff know that Mueller sent thank yous and updates to his donors telling of the wonderful things God was doing? Though he did not *ask*, he thanked donors and kept them informed. I highly respect George Mueller because he reminds me to look to God. Unfortunately, the Evangelical public worldwide has elevated George Mueller's no-ask practice into the *spiritual way* to fundraise, which confuses thousands of missionaries even to this day. Is it possible that Mueller's accidental popularity has done more harm than good?

Alma and I tried Mueller's model and found it didn't work. Because we didn't have enough faith? Possibly, but more likely it is because we needed to exercise even *more* faith by inviting others to join us.

For a history on how Mueller arrived at his no-ask convictions check my book, *Funding Your Ministry* at Navpress.com.

What about *hinting*?

A prayer request at the bottom of your newsletter asking readers to *pray about your support* might generate a few one-off gifts. Asking people to *pray about your trip* to Taiwan might also raise a little money. Perhaps we have trained our donors to understand that "please pray" means "please give!"

Hinting is most common where gospel workers can't get up the nerve to make a genuine ask. If they merely hint, they do not feel as rejected when donors ignore the hint. After all, they didn't really *ask*.

Secondly, hinting reveals shallowness in the relationship between asker and giver. Not having confidence in our relationship with a donor, we withhold an honest appeal. We cannot share our hearts for fear of ruining the friendship.

Thirdly, hinting could show that I don't think the donor has the ability to handle a forthright invitation to join my vision. It devalues him as a person.

In other areas of ministry we do not hint. Do you hint when you ask someone to receive Christ?

Even if your conscience or your culture says asking is wrong, the Bible says differently. For example:

- The Apostle Paul appealed for the church in Jerusalem (2 Corinthians 8:10–11).

  "I give my opinion in this matter...who were the first to begin a year ago not only to do this, but also to desire to do it. But now finish doing it also..."

- Paul appealed for his own support (Romans 15:20–24).

  "...whenever I go to Spain —for I hope to see you in passing and to be helped [propempo] on my way there by you..."

- Jesus expected the 12 disciples to ask "worthy men" to host them.

  "And whatever city or village you enter, inquire who is worthy in it, and stay at his house until you leave that city." (Matthew 10:11)

- Joash, Moses, Nehemiah, Elijah, and Hezekiah invited people to give generously to advance God's Kingdom.

Your staff might have high visibility and communicate well, and even do holy hinting, but those culs-de-sac will take them in circles. Visibility and communications *cost* money. Asking *raises* money! Honor potential partners by giving them opportunities one by one to make serious stewardship decisions.

TAKEAWAY:

- Are any of your staff stuck in the three culs-de-sac—hoping that information, visibility, or hinting will raise funds?
- How about you?
- What "non-hinting" but sensitive words can you and your staff use when you ask?

Warn your staff about a fourth cul-de-sac: The saying "Money follows ministry" has been around for years—that is, if you faithfully minister to people, they will support you financially without an appeal. There is a biblical precedent here:

- Jesus was supported by those to whom he ministered (Luke 8:1–3).
- Believers were to support their teachers (Galatians 6:6, 1 Corinthians 9:11).

Fair enough. But did these followers give without an appeal? Don't know. Nevertheless, how encouraging when those to whom we have ministered start giving without our asking—"They just started without me doing a thing! Thank God."

But that is the exception. Many believers today do not know this principle. How many gospel workers are waiting in vain for those they have led in Bible study to start supporting them?

You still need to ask.

SECTION
THREE

Your Strategies: Blind Spots In Your
Fundraising Practices

You and your team have spent a few days in retreat at Dream Lake eating cookies and dreaming about the future. You've scribbled new plans on flipcharts based on your team's vision and values. You have fresh, exciting strategies for the work God has given you, and even a timetable.

This is an enjoyable part of leadership—planning, dreaming, and creating.

But your work is not yet finished. How are you going to pay for these dreams? How will you lead your team in fundraising as you move forward from Dream Lake? For example:

- *Do you have a wise funding plan that includes face to face appeals?*

- *What is the strategy to minister to major donors?*

- *In your communications do you treat donors like ATMs or true partners?*

- *Are you presenting a bold vision or pleading for your needs?*

As a leader you must understand that how you ask and how you treat your giving partners is an important part of leadership. What happens after you come back from Dream Lake?

The Missing Link in Leadership Planning

WISE LEADERS PERIODICALLY TAKE THEIR TEAMS off-site to pray, evaluate, and plan. Flipchart sheets are taped to the walls, philosophical questions are debated, 80 dozen chocolate chip cookies are devoured (the first day) and friendships are deepened. Even the ever-cautious accountants seem to enjoy it.

Planning retreats build vision and teamwork, one of the best things a leader can do. But don't let your team go home unless these two questions are resolved:

1. *This grand vision we worked on for three days, what will it cost?*

2. *How will we find the money?*

A major donor officer says it this way:

> *The leaders retreat to the lake and dream great dreams. The next week they slip a note under my door with a number on it — the amount of money they need to accomplish their dreams and a date by when they need it. But it makes me feel small. I am expected to invite donors to give sacrificially to a vision I had no part in creating and barely understand.*

Actually, he has never had a note slipped under his door, but that is how it feels. Overstated? No.

Back to Moses: He had his own 40 day "off-site" meeting at Mt. Sinai. But one thing was different: *The funding strategy and the ministry strategy were given together.*

When Moses got the plan from God for *building* the tabernacle (Exodus 25–35), he also received the plan for *funding* it — invite the Israelites to give. God even gave a 14 item list of what was needed: gold, silver, ram's skins, linen, porpoise skins to name five. Quite detailed.

Similarly, Nehemiah included a financial action step in his plan to rebuild Jerusalem. He asked the king for timber with which to build.

PRINCIPLE:

Planning for your vision is not complete without a funding plan assembled by those who are expected to help carry it out.

However, it is easy to neglect the final step of planning — *funding*. Instead leaders say:

- *Development will do it*

- *Let's just start — God will provide*

- *Tighten our belts, do more with less*

- *Borrow*

- *The Bill Gates Foundation!*

During your blue sky meetings, dream as if there are no financial limitations. Don't let a scarcity mentality limit you. But before you leave, ask:

How are we going to pay for all this blue sky?

We! Funding is not the leader's job alone. Does your team feel the financial burden along with you?

It is difficult to create a funding plan if you don't first create a budget. And you can't create a meaningful budget if the plans are too ethereal. This is where many leaders struggle. They lack the patience to develop the detail planning from which a budget can be written.

For example, they might say: "We dare to open 10 new outposts in the next three years." Great, but now we need details — the costs for salaries, housing, transport, office rent. The funding plan arises from these details. Do the homework necessary to know how much you'll need to raise and by when.

Your vision casting is not finished until you've addressed the budget and the fundraising, and don't address it in a vacuum. Bring to the meetings selected fundraising and accounting staff, maybe even a key donor or two. Involve them deeply in the planning process.

It is not a solution to assume that a major donor will automatically pick up the tab. Think harder with your team.

Don't come down the mountain (or back from Dream Lake) and slip a note under the fundraising guy's door. If you don't have a fundraising guy, you will have to slip the note under your own door!

TAKEAWAY

- Which accounting and fundraising staff should join your planning sessions as valued participants (not merely observers)?
- Has your team actually prayed together about your funding plans?
- Have you identified specific major donors to invite to partner in planning these dreams?
- Assign action steps for each staff for the fundraising strategy— everyone helps lift the load, even the introverted accountants.
- Should a few giving partners join you at Dream Lake so they can better own the vision? Are the fundraisers at Dream Lake? Should be!

What I do at planning meetings:

I use this agenda:

- What is our mission? What are we trying to do?
- What is our current reality—the way things are now? What's going well? Not so well? Are we accomplishing our mission?
- What is our desired future reality—the way things ought to be? Any external circumstances to capitalize on?
- What three-five future reality changes should we make? (Can't make 25 all at once!)
- What's our action plan?
- What will the plan cost—our budget?

- How will we fund it? Use "Appendix G: Project Pyramid" to get started on the fundraising plan. Leave plenty of time for this discussion. Don't leave it for the last 30 minutes.

What I learned about fundraising action steps:

I always write the funding goal on the flipchart or whiteboard. Don't underestimate the power of all the players seeing it in writing at the same time. Then I list the fundraising tactics with a date for completion, including names of donors with a suggested amount by each name for all to discuss. Then we pray.

One Thing Leaders Must Not Delegate

THIS LESSON COMES FROM THE YEAR 800 B.C. via the little known story of Judah's boy-king, Joash. When Joash was a baby, his power hungry grandmother, Athaliah, seized control of the throne in Jerusalem and desecrated the temple to worship the Baals.

> *Now when Athaliah the mother of Ahaziah saw that her son [Ahaziah] was dead, she rose and destroyed all the royal offspring of the house of Judah. (2 Chronicles 22:10)*

Athaliah *killed her grandchildren* to eliminate future heirs to the throne — killed her grandchildren! But she overlooked baby Joash who was hidden by his older sister.

When Joash turned seven, the high priest, Jehoiada, furtively organized a palace coup. They secretly put the crown on little Joash's head and shouted, "Long live the king!"

When Queen Athaliah heard the celebration, she rushed into the courtyard shouting, "Treason! Treason!" But by prearranged plan, the Levites seized her and put her to death. Judah now had a seven year old king under the tutelage of the high priest, Jehoiada.

Years passed. The temple remained in disrepair for all to see.

When King Joash grew to manhood, he courageously decided to restore the long neglected house of God. To finance the building campaign, he ordered the Levites (full-time temple workers) to collect the half shekel Moses had commanded 600 years earlier for the desert tabernacle. He told them:

> *Go out to the cities of Judah and collect money from all Israel to*

*repair the house of your God annually, and you shall do the matter quickly. **But the Levites did not act quickly.** (2 Chronicles 24:5, emphasis mine)*

His *Fundraising Team* failed. Not to be stopped, Joash bored a hole in the top of a chest, displayed it at the gate and exhorted the Jews to give Moses's half-shekel to repair the temple. They willingly gave — a successful campaign.

What is the lesson for leaders today?

Do not delegate your fundraising responsibility. As a leader, you have a unique platform that inspires staff and donors alike. Don't squander your leadership by abdicating.

Unfortunately, it is not that easy. One CEO told me: "Everyone thinks *his issue* should be number one on my crowded agenda — and now you want me to take 30 percent of my time for major donor fundraising? Impossible."

At the risk of oversimplification, ask your supervisor or board to help you reorganize to free you up for fundraising. Delegate administrative details, *but don't abdicate*. Like Joash, *own* your fundraising responsibility.

PRINCIPLE:

Leaders can delegate many things, but they must not delegate their responsibility for fundraising. Fundraising is part of the leadership role.

Too many leaders wish they could magically fulfill their fundraising duties by getting on an airplane once a year to join a funding specialist in taking a mega-donor to dinner in a distant city. The money guy does all the "relationship stuff" before and after. The leader shows up for the appeal, then jumps back on the airplane and returns to his *leadership* role.

Dr. Diana Kuntz, president and CEO of the Volunteers of America, presents a refreshing partnership with her development staff:

"I've asked my development director to manage me, tell me when my help is necessary and where I can be the most useful."[6]

Kuntz meets with her development team *weekly* to plan fundraising action steps.

You need not manage the day to day funding activities of your team, but like Joash you must provide an *emotional rallying point.* Donors need to see your face, hear your voice, and feel your passion. If you resent spending time with donors, they sense that.

In similar fashion, your staff must hear about your fundraising activities because it gives them permission to do the same. If you never talk about fundraising, your staff assume it is not a high value.

Final thought:

You have the right to ask your staff about their funding activities — the way Joash asked Jehoiada, *"Why have you not required the Levites to bring...the levy fixed by Moses?" (2 Chronicles 24:6).* No answer is recorded. This was likely an awkward moment for Jehoiada.

Gospel workers generally do not volunteer information about their fundraising activities, so you must ask. Even if it is awkward for them or you. Like King Joash, ask!

TAKEAWAY

- What must change so you will have more time to think about and do fundraising?

- Who can help you—your Development Director? A successful funding specialist? Be cautious about taking advice from a non-fundraiser. Be especially cautious about taking advice from successful business leaders who are good at sales and think they can save you. It is not the same.

- Is it time to ask your staff the Joash-Jehoiada question, "Why are you not working on fundraising?"

- What tips you off that you are abdicating your fundraising role? For example, avoiding donor phone calls, not reading funding reports, not initiating appointments?

- With whom can you safely discuss this?

Let's be practical (I know you are swamped):

Start with ten! Ask your administrative team to bring you the top 50 current donors in your country in descending order of gift size. With your development team and other leaders review them one by one. Identify the ten for which you will be the point person for communication and making appeals. Only ten.

Ask the development team and your leadership team to sort out who will take responsibility for others.

For you, start with ten. Take a look at Appendix D.

Do You Present Needs or Vision?

EMERGENCY APPEALS CAN RAISE A TON of money. Donors gladly bail you out once or twice. But don't be seduced. They won't rescue you 12 times a year. Donors want to touch lives, not rescue you or erase deficits or pay your kids' orthodontist bills month after month.

Instead of asking for your needs, ask for your vision. Help your giving partners visualize how their money will be used — to provide clean water for a village, to sponsor a sick child in Uganda, to enable a campus ministry rep to reach a wayward student.

Avoid the word "need." You don't have a *need* to be funded, you have a *vision* to be accomplished. You are not looking for charitable handouts to get you through the month. You are inviting partners to join you in building God's Kingdom. Be vision driven, not need driven.

Use this diagram to determine if you are primarily vision driven or need driven:

Appeal Element	Need Driven	Vision Driven
Explain cause	Budget or needs presented	Opportunity presented
Compelling words	Frantic, need money now	Change a life
Theme	*What* we do, activities	*Why* we do it, tell story
Threat in appeal	Our mission will wither if we don't get money	If vision is unfulfilled, lives will not be changed

Appeal Element	Need Driven	Vision Driven
Giving is	A Transaction	An investment in "our" joint vision
Emotions	Bail us out!	Touch lives together

Need driven fundraising produces cash for the short term, but donors eventually feel used. Emergency after emergency gives donors the impression you are a bad planner. Vision driven fundraising invites joyful, generous partners to own the vision with you.

PRINCIPLE:

Biblical fundraising is not about getting charitable gifts to meet your needs but attracting loyal partners to join your vision.

To help your staff move from need driven to vision driven fundraising, review with them Paul's 4 P's outline for his ministry to Spain in Romans 15:20–24:

Paul's Passion (v 20)

And thus I aspired to preach the gospel, not where Christ was already named...

To preach where Christ is not named inspires action. Paul intends to take the gospel to Spain (verse 24), the end of the then-known world. That's more inspiring than, "Help me meet my budget."

And notice how simply Paul states his passion — 14 words. A veteran missionary was invited to share a five minute ministry update at our Sunday school class, but he balked. He needed "at least thirty minutes" to explain his vision. Hmmm. My leader friend, you know a lot, but you must condense. The more you know about a subject the more difficult it is to articulate it meaningfully and succinctly.

Paul's Promise (v 21)

Paul quotes Isaiah 52:15:

...but as it is written, "They who had no news of Him shall see, And they who have not heard shall understand."

Where did Paul get his passion to preach all the way to Gibraltar? Obviously, from his conversion on the Damascus road where Christ charged him to "bear my name before the Gentiles" (Acts 9:15). But verse 21 reveals a second motivation — a promise from the Old Testament that helped explain the *why* of Paul's passion.

Paul's Partnership Appeal (v 24)

...for I hope to see you in passing and to be helped on my way there by you...

"Helped on my way" is the Greek *propempo* — a strong word rooted in Middle Eastern hospitality. It means "practical assistance" (*Vine's Dictionary of New Testament Words*). Two thousand years later we don't understand *propempo* like the Romans would have. Paul is not asking for a rah-rah pie supper send-off to Spain. The Romans clearly understood Paul was inviting their support to advance the gospel in Spain.

Paul's Personal Relationships (vv 24 and 32)

...when I have first enjoyed your company for a while...

...find refreshing rest in your company.

Fundraising is more than getting money. We are recruiting *ministry partners*, and that starts with unhurried face to face meetings.

Paul's 4 P's outline can be used effectively in any culture. Try it yourself and guide your staff through the 4 P's.

- *Passion:* Share with enthusiasm the vision God has given you.

- *Promise:* Tell how God called you to this passion — including your scriptural promise.

- *Partnership:* Propempo. Tell potential giving partners you can't do it alone. Invite them to partner with you in accomplishing your vision.

- *Personal relationships:* Enjoy their company for a while.

TAKEAWAY

- Which of your staff are stuck on needs based fundraising? Discuss this chapter with them.
- Ask your staff:
  - What promise of Scripture undergirds your passion?
  - Asking—what exactly do you say? Can you improve it?
  - What can you do to "enjoy their company" and help giving partners enjoy yours?
  - How can you more effectively articulate the passion God has given you for an official presentation? For a 30 second elevator speech?
  - From the chart above, are you presenting needs or vision?

A Personal Lesson from Kentucky:

An elderly couple from Kentucky had generously supported The Navigators for years, but no one had thanked them in person. It was time for a visit.

As I drove my airport rental car from St. Louis to their home in Paducah, I wondered if they were just being nice to give me an appointment. I determined not to take too much of their time and hoped to get back to St. Louis before nightfall. And I was in a hurry, as per usual.

After a leisurely two hour lunch at their country club, they invited me to "see the town." Hmmm. St. Louis by nightfall? Probably not. So all over Paducah we went, talking, laughing and finding "refreshing rest in each other's company." When I asked about their spiritual journey, they shared their hearts. A bond was formed as we prayed together at the end of an enjoyable afternoon.

My 'short' visit to Paducah lasted five hours, and yes, I made an appeal. But the highlight was their asking for the scripture memory packet I'd described in my spiritual journey. They wanted to grow in Christ. I learned a valuable lesson about slowing down and enjoying people. A few months later they gave a five figure gift for our capital campaign.

Giving Partners or ATMs?

HAVE YOU SEEN THE HUMOROUS BILLBOARD of a smiling lady with gorgeous white teeth? The caption reads: *Ignore your teeth and they'll go away.* In leadership fundraising we need a billboard with a smiling giving partner saying: *Ignore your donors and they'll go away.*

You have two ministries, first to the people you touch as a leader and second to your giving partners. Both are equally important, but I observe that most gospel workers spend 98 percent of their time in field ministry and only two percent with giving partners.

As you increase leadership responsibility, you'll need to raise more than your personal budget — you may need a city budget, a regional budget, an intern staff budget, and a Director's Initiative Fund. That means spending more time in fundraising and donor ministry. Don't be a typical overly busy leader adding funding on top of your other responsibilities but not dropping anything.

I use the term *donor ministry* rather than the popular phrase *donor maintenance*. Our giving partners are not databases to be maintained. They are vulnerable human beings who need encouragement. They are not emotionless ATMs, but people who long to come closer to Christ.

Read between the lines in Nehemiah's relationship with King Artaxerxes. Nehemiah was a lowly cupbearer, but Artaxerxes knew Nehemiah well enough to ask, "Why is your face sad?" That implies a deep respectful relationship, and that took time.

By now you realize that fundraising is more than asking. Unfortunately, some leaders connect with donors only when funds are needed.

This diagram presents an idealized but instructive model in the spirit of Philippians 4:17–"not that I seek the gift itself".

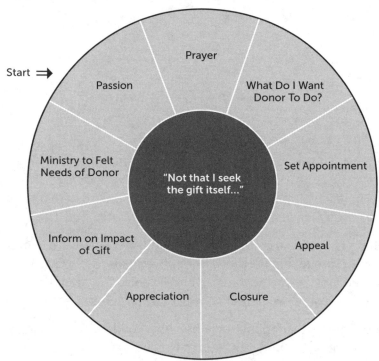

Notice that the appeal (lower right side) is only one of several interactions. Depending on the relationship, you might appeal more or less frequently. My point: Don't make an appeal every time.

PRINCIPLE:

Those who contribute to your ministry are living human beings who are partners in your work. They deserve more than a token amount of attention.

Remember also, major donors give to fund *their* dreams, not yours. Ask them, "What kinds of things do you like to give to?" Being a nice person who traveled 400 miles to visit them might generate a token gift, but they won't give *major* gifts just because they like you.

Additionally, when donors fall on hard times and reduce their giving, continue the friendship lest you communicate that you value only their money.

Can donor ministry be delegated to the development team or to a funding specialist? Some administrative details and record keeping can certainly be delegated, but major donors want to talk to the leader. Nehemiah did not send his messenger Hanini to appeal to Artaxerxes.

It's impossible for busy leaders to relate to all donors equally, so you must focus on a few — the right few. This is where you and your development team or your fundraising guru must work together. Start with ten donors or potential donors for whom you are the point person.

Another way to minister to your partners is to involve them in your work. Moses is a good example. With his call for funding also came the call to participate manually.

> *Let every skillful man among you come, and make all that the LORD has commanded. (Exodus 35:10)*

When possible, give your partners a piece of the ministry action. Give them the thrill of involvement, and they will never leave you.

How much time should a leader spend in fundraising and donor ministry? In the past I hesitated to give a percentage because I didn't want to be legalistic, but my spiritualized stonewalling helped no one. Today, at the risk of oversimplification, I suggest 20 percent minimum. If you are the CEO, or if you lead a city or region, then 30–40 percent.

I once asked a leader of a booming worldwide ministry (whose name you would recognize) how much time he devoted to fundraising. I was not surprised when he replied, "Fifty percent."

I realize this 20–50% talk blows your leadership paradigm. Please don't reject my suggestions merely because your organization has no history of spending this much time in funding. Non-profits that are healthy year after year have leaders who spend tons of time in fundraising.

Rob Mahon, Ministry Director in Albuquerque, New Mexico spends 30 percent of his time in fundraising/donor ministry. He says, "Donors want to hear about ministry progress from the director — me."

He "owns" the city budget which includes his support, new ministry programs, and *timber* for 25 diverse staff. By working together, they are all fully funded by December 31 of each year.

Typically, when leaders get busy, fundraising is dropped. Just last week a godly leader wrote, "The agenda for this meeting has become a traffic jam so we will skip the fundraising report." What? Drop something else!

I am not suggesting you work longer hours. Instead, cut something from your schedule. Can't cut? Look at your job description through donor eyes. Ask your board, your spouse, and your funding coach to help.

To move toward spending more time in fundraising, finish the sentences below: "I'd spend more time in funding and donor ministry if I..."

- Knew specifically what to do

- Could delegate some of my other work

- Considered the funding of ministry just as important as my other work

- Could keep my schedule free from constant emergencies

- Wasn't intimidated by major donors

- Had an administrative assistant

- Could get more help from the development team

- Other_____

Which one(s) is the Lord speaking to you about? With whom can you discuss this?

TAKEAWAY

- Who are the top ten potential major donors you will take responsibility to communicate with, minister to, and appeal to? Use "Appendix D: Top Ten National Partners" or download it from scottmorton.net.

- Who can help you review your workload to find time for donor ministry?

- What percentage of time do your staff spend in fundraising/donor ministry? Discuss the questions above with them.

What helped me get from two percent to 20 percent?

As a married mission leader with two kids, it occurred to me that I had made bigger promises to my wife than I had to my ministry. I realized I was setting my family up to resent ministry because we were always broke. So I started putting more time into fundraising, and I delegated more to my administrative assistant and traveled less. Surprise: The work thrived and so did our funding. And our home became a more joyful place.

Is Giving Intellectual or Emotional?

HOW WOULD YOUR STAFF ANSWER?

I used to say *intellectual*, but I changed my mind after writing national direct mail appeals. I quickly learned that intellect and logic alone do not inspire givers nearly as much as logic *plus* emotion. People make giving decisions with their hearts.

Moses' tabernacle givers were those with "stirred hearts."

> *Everyone whose heart stirred him and everyone whose spirit moved him came and brought the LORD'S contribution... (Exodus 35:21–22)*

I'm not suggesting you bypass people's minds, far from it. But think a minute: you live 24/7 in a world of mission strategy. Your staff discussions about "organic maximization in the 10/40 window" excite you, but would sound goofy to outsiders. If your fundraising appeal is a theological treatise or missiology meandering, you'll put donors to sleep.

Sadly, leaders often wax eloquently about mission strategy or demographics in their fundraising. That background study must be done, and with some foundations, churches or boards it must be presented. But donors don't make giving decisions based primarily on your research.

A few years ago I was logically pontificating to a potential donor on the benefits of our youth camping ministry in the mountains. She listened patiently but seemed bored. I was panicking. When I finally invited her to give she said, "You had me when you told about that kid from an abusive home."

I stumbled into a successful appeal! I was focused on logic, but I accidentally touched this donor's heart through a story about a teen from an abusive home.

PRINCIPLE:

People make giving decisions (and many of life's decisions) spurred by emotion, not intellect alone. Emotion can be produced through the power of a story,

How do you bring emotion to your presentations? Get out of your office and search for how broken lives are repaired through your organization, and then plainly describe it. Tell your story the way it actually happens on the street.

If that doesn't produce emotion, you've got bad fact gathering, mediocre writing, bland storytelling, and maybe all three. As my wizened Journalism 201 professor, Dr. Kunerth, used to say, "There is no such thing as a dull subject, but there are dull writers." And I might add, "dull askers!"

My partner in ministry, Dave Gresham, has learned that major donors primarily want to know
two things:

1. Are people coming to Christ?

2. Are lives being changed by Christ?

To stir hearts:

- Spend hours on Mt. Sinai figuring out what God is saying to you.

- Spend hours in the grassroots with your staff and the people who receive your ministry.

- Test what you say with donors. Learn what piques their interest.

- Capsulize your work by developing a few simple stories about real people in the grassroots.

Can appeals be too emotional? Yes. Haven't we grown callous to heartrending appeals for needy orphans, needy firemen, and needy homeless people? Some organizations need to tone it down, but others need to pep it up. Help your donors visualize how their gifts touch one life. People give to people.

TAKEAWAY:

- Do you and your staff's fundraising appeals speak primarily to hearts or to intellects?
- What is it about your mission that stirs emotions?
- Do your "stories" stretch the truth?
- Do your staff know how to tell heart stories?
- How can you pass your vision on to the next generation? Not white papers, but storytelling. What stories do you and your staff tell over and over?

What I do in storytelling:

Telling heart touching stories need not be difficult. As a model, here is a true story I have used describing my city ministry.

I was never sure if A wanted to continue our Bible meetings. Maybe he was only being polite. Nevertheless, I stopped at the corner Burger King near his house at 6:45 a.m. for three breakfast sandwiches, one for A, his son, and me.

The house was dark as I rang the doorbell of the small duplex, but out popped his son on the way to school. I tossed him a sandwich. Then it was just A and me sitting in the dark eating our breakfast. He had but one small lamp.

A was only 30, but he had suffered plenty—an absent father in Miami, a history of drinking and partying, a wife who played around while he was in the military in Germany. Now he was in charge of the kids. We had been meeting for this early morning study in

John's gospel for eight months. He had tons of questions I didn't answer very well. On this particular morning A seemed thoughtful. "What was coming?" I wondered.

Finally he asked, "Do you think a person could do business with God during a smoke break at work?" (He worked the night shift at a manufacturing company.)

"Yes," I said. "Sure."

A continued, "I went out for a smoke on the company patio last night and started talking to God. I started crying, and I couldn't stop. Something happened." He looked up at me. His eyes were misty and he was smiling broadly. "Something happened," he repeated.

Please pray for A. He has entered into life with Christ. He has so many difficulties, but something has happened! And we are praying this will happen over and over around our city.

What makes a good story?

- Detail—the listener must be able to visualize you standing at the door at 6:45.

- No rambling. Be succinct.

- Build suspense. Describe your fears. "I was never sure if A wanted to continue our Bible meetings." Tell about a "lion roaring in the distance."

- Tell it just like it happened.

- Don't give away the ending until the end.

Our model for storytelling—Jesus! We still have His parables. People remember stories.

Loyalty Schmoyalty

IN YEARS PAST, GIVING PARTNERS GAVE heavily out of loyalty to their church or nonprofits. But those days are passing.

Today, you cannot rely on organizational reputation or history, even if it is sterling. You must say more than, "Support us. We did good work in the past." Today's givers, from millennials to boomers, are picky. They want to see your passion. Their money goes to those organizations that solve people-problems. They support *causes* that touch their hearts and make a difference, not sterile institutions.

They also want to see *outcomes* — is their giving creating spiritual dividends?

How do busy leaders explain their cause in compelling, inspiring ways? Nehemiah offers an insight.

When Nehemiah heard the current reality of Jerusalem he "wept and mourned for many days" (Nehemiah 1:4). News from the field stoked Nehemiah's fire.

Similarly today, seek news from the troubled city. Talk with people in the grassroots. Go to the street! Talk with those who receive your organization's help — even those who reject your help. You'll come back with deeper convictions about your mission and a bucketful of ideas on how to make your message more compelling.

As National Development Director, I took our team on three day field trips each year to interact with field workers to rekindle our enthusiasm.

How can you best *articulate* your mission? Unfortunately, many leaders assume they are naturally articulate, spellbinding communicators. Sorry. Even if you are a good speaker, these four disciplines can help you be more compelling:

- *What problem are you trying to solve? Whom will you help?* Be specific. Don't say, "Relieve suffering." Rather, "to bring gospel hope and affordable housing to the devastated Southside Communities." Don't try to solve nine problems, just one or two.

PRINCIPLE:

Most people today give, not out of blind loyalty to an organization, but toward causes that inspire them and for which they can identify specific outcomes.

- *Are you succinct?* Nehemiah used only sixteen words, "Send me to Judah, to the city of my fathers' tombs, that I may rebuild it." Build your *case statement* (to use philanthropy language) by first writing down *one vision sentence* — just one! Then let the words stare back at you. Rewrite it. Show it to others. Even better, show it to your spouse. Boil down your many ideas. Dawson Trotman, Founder of The Navigators, said:

"Thoughts disentangle themselves when passed through the lips or pencil tips."

- *Do you use ministry lingo?* The in-house ministry lingo you and your staff toss around daily makes sense to you, but it's a mystery to giving partners. Speaking to donors in *your* language rather than theirs smacks of arrogance and laziness. Stop it.

- *Are you speaking in word pictures?* Nehemiah didn't say the J-word, Jerusalem. Why remind Artaxerxes of his former enemy? Instead he used the emotional word picture, "city of my fathers' tombs." If you have buried your father, you understand.

Former radio host Paul Ramsier of KTIS in Minneapolis was an effective communicator but had only his voice — no video. He told me his secret at a National Radio Broadcasters convention. "As you speak, does your listener visualize actors and scenery on the stage of her mind? If not, you are merely throwing words at her. She will switch to an oldies station."

Similarly, when you articulate your vision, what scenery and actors jump onstage in your listeners' minds?

Merely quoting your organizational mission statement will not motivate donors. Though it was labored over for hours by dedicated staff, it is *cold* to outsiders who were not involved in creating it.

A second motivating factor for today's donors is outcomes. What are the visible results of your work?

Organizations vacillate between two extremes. On one side are those who say you can't measure God's work or you can't measure how deeply lives are touched, so they are vague about outcomes. For example, "Your support enabled us to touch the lives of countless military personnel last year."

On the other extreme, some organizations present details about exactly how many came to Christ, exactly how many were fed in the soup kitchen, exactly how many hits were recorded to their website. For example, "Your support enabled us to enroll 2,156 military personnel (and spouses) in beginning Bible studies last year. Of those, 812 signed a card saying they had trusted Christ for the first time."

Which do you like better? Which do your giving partners prefer?

In my experience, I find leaders generally reluctant to specifically identify what donors' gifts will accomplish. I get that. What if they can't perform what they promised? But givers are not impressed with hedging and vague generalities.

Sadly, some leaders know what they want to accomplish specifically, but they haven't done the homework of matching money to results. They want new staff, but they have not figured out how many new staff could be added if $89,000 came in, and where would they be placed. It is more exciting to dream about good stuff happening than to record those dreams in the form of specific outcomes. Don't pin me down.

But today's donors want outcomes — not down to the eyelash, but with enough details so they can visualize how their hard-earned dollars, pesos, or shillings are being used.

TAKEAWAY

- Using the four questions above, how can you make your presentations more compelling?

- Do you need to "go to the street" to get first-hand stories?

- Are you satisfied with the way your staff communicate organizational vision?

- Does your organizational website or literature inspire others? Does it inspire you?

- In your appeals in print or in person, do you articulate potential outcomes? Rate your organization on the "vague to specific" extremes.

Bold Vision But Chicken-Out Asking

WHEN YOUR STAFF MAKE FUNDRAISING APPEALS, do they ask boldly? Or do they "chicken-out?" (as we say in America).

The secret is not using magic words or taking the donor to a nice restaurant. The secret is passion. If you and your staff truly believe in your vision, you will not be (indeed, you cannot be) an apologetic asker.

Consider these stinging words from Jesus Film founder Paul Eshelmann:

> *"If you are unwilling to do fundraising for your vision then I question whether you truly believe in your vision. You only believe in what you are willing to raise funds for."*

Wow!

One trait of the six biblical leaders we are looking at pops to the surface like a fishing bobber on a placid sunfish pond — They had *bold vision* and they made *bold appeals.*

Bold appeals — not obnoxious appeals! You can find obnoxious prosperity gospel askers on late night American TV and daytime Nigerian TV where "riches will come your way if you plant a seed gift." Bold does not mean abrasive or manipulative. But it does involve risk. For example:

* Though "very much afraid," Nehemiah boldly appealed to a Persian king who could have killed him for breaching royal protocols (Nehemiah 2:2).

- Moses risked alienating his people by asking them to give the precious possessions they brought from Egypt.

- Paul risked rejection from the fledgling Gentile churches by exhorting them to support Jewish leaders 500 miles away in Jerusalem.

Bold asking does not mean putting pressure on your potential donor. Your goal is to inspire her to bring your appeal *before the Lord* to make a *stewardship decision*. How to get her to take your appeal seriously? Face to face. Sit up straight. Make sure you have her attention. Pause. Look her in the eye. Ask her to pray about a specific gift or range. Then stop!

You will need to rehearse.

Appealing by text or letter doesn't require as much boldness.

If your staff say "Bold appeals won't work in my situation" or "Our people can't afford to give," ask them, "Is your situation more difficult than Moses'?"

Moses' potential donors were in a vast wilderness, possessing only a few belongings and what the Egyptians gave them as they fled Egypt. But Moses boldly listed fourteen items needed for the tabernacle; gold, silver, linen, even water repellent porpoise skins.

I have taught mission leaders around the world to make bold appeals, and the results are similar in every culture. After being trained (and rehearsing with a friend) in asking for support face to face, they receive a yes 50–70% of the time — even in the *indirect* cultures of Asia. There is no substitute.

Your people can't afford to give? If they have even a small income, they have the privilege of giving (Deuteronomy 16:17). Beware of the 'limited pie' scarcity view, which says, "If I take a big piece of pie, there is more for me and less for you." Is there a shortage of resources in God's wide world? No. Only a shortage of passionate ideas and bold askers.

To help your team grow in making dynamite bold face to face appeals, try these ideas.

1. Thoroughly train your staff to skilfully make bold appeals. Send them for training even if they have been before.

2. Go with them on a couple of appeals. Before you leave, ask the staff: "What do you want this potential donor to do, specifically?" Don't be vague. Roleplay the appeal together.

3. Remind them to beware of seeking outwardly affluent donors. In *The Millionaire Next Door* Thomas J. Stanley and William D. Danko remind us:

   Most of the truly wealthy in [America] don't live in Beverly Hills or on Park Avenue — they live next door.

   And:

   Many people who display a high consumption lifestyle have little or no investments [or] appreciable assets.

   Most millionaires don't look rich. Those who look rich are often driving their wealth, wearing their wealth, or sailing on their wealth. They have little to give even though they dress well for church.

   This is not merely an American phenomenon. Mission leaders from around the world tell me that a "poor looking" friend surprised them with generous support, and that "rich looking" donors gave but little.

   Don't be quick to judge who can and cannot give. Boldly ask potential partners to give sacrificially no matter how they "look."

4. Ask your staff if they truly believe in their vision. Do they merely quote the company line? If they cannot be passionate about your organization's mission,

> **PRINCIPLE:**
> Biblical leaders possess bold vision, and because they are impassioned by it, they make bold funding appeals.

can they be passionate about a portion of it — a specialty division within your organization? Or a different mission?

Fundraising is not about getting your need met or your organization's need met. My Kenyan teaching partner, Noel Owuor, says it this way:

Fundraising is not asking people to help you pay for groceries or school fees. It is about advancing the gospel. Fundraising is a gospel issue.

What helps me to be bold?

Rehearsing. I discipline myself to ask, "What exactly do I want this potential donor to do?" Then I run through three or four scenarios of what I will say in my appeal and settle on the best one.

Secondly, I anticipate questions. That honors the donor. Even Nehemiah had a Q and A session with Artaxerxes and his wife (Nehemiah 2:6), and Nehemiah was ready.

Thirdly, at the right time, I just blurt it out! "To do all that God is calling me to do I must have a few people to anchor the financial team. May I ask you to consider $15,000 to $20,000 for this ministry project?" Then I stop talking!

TAKEAWAY

- Be yourself. You can be bold without morphing into a reality TV host.

- Stop hinting. Merely talking about the project and hoping the donor gives wastes time and dishonors the Lord, you, and the donor. Look her in the eye, be courteous and direct.

- Don't look on the outward appearance (1 Samuel 16:7). If they "look like they have money" they probably don't. Give everyone an opportunity.

- Have you asked your staff: "Why are you apologetic?"

Send Money. I'll Explain Later...

IN FUNDRAISING, LEADERS NEED TO COME down from the mountain a few steps. Though they eloquently describe their vision with soaring phrases, they struggle to be specific in asking.

Recently a rookie development officer for a homeless shelter invited a local major donor to tour their downtown facility. The tour went well and the generous benefactor seemed pleased. It was now time to make "the ask." The development officer fumbled for words, but he finally asked the generous friend to "give something that would be meaningful to you."

The next day the donor called back and asked, "What exactly did you want from me?" The nervous fundraiser said, "T-t-t-twenty thousand." The donor replied, "Yes. I will give $20,000 for the project — $10,000 in cash and $10,000 in advice. Here is the advice. 'Always ask for what you want.'" [1]

Bible leaders also asked *specifically*.

- Nehemiah — timber to rebuild Jerusalem's walls, visa documents for safe passage

- Joash — the half-shekel poll tax to rebuild the temple

- Hezekiah — tithe to empower Levitical teachers

But most specific is Moses. To construct the tabernacle he requested fourteen items, including porpoise skins (Exodus 35:4–9).

What if Moses had said, "Give something that would be meaningful to you?" Listing specific items helped each person decide what he could give. The poor desert donor with nothing to give except a meager waterproof porpoise skin could visualize his gift shielding the tabernacle from occasional desert downpours. He too participated in the work of God.

A generous friend, Margaret from Wisconsin, advised me, "Scott, tell the mission workers to be specific! From the appeals I receive I don't know if they want $25 per month or $2,500 cash or prayer support or to borrow my car. Tell them to be honest with me, and I'll be honest with them."

PRINCIPLE:

Ask specifically for what will help you accomplish your vision. Don't be vague.

No matter what your culture, don't ignore Margaret's advice. Donors like specifics — even the indirect cultures of Asia. It's human nature. Tell the truth!

A local charity phoned recently to say their truck was coming to our neighborhood for donations. "What do you need?" I asked, puzzled. "Used clothing or canned vegetables," the caller immediately answered. Without that specific suggestion we would not have known what to do and might have done nothing.

However, your suggested amounts should not be numbers picked out of the air. They must have a basis — like sponsoring a day of ministry, funding a student pizza supper or a line item in your budget. Give it prayerful thought.

A leader told me a few years ago, "Help me with words. What do I actually *say* in my appeal?" Okay, here are some 'words' to get you started. Recalibrate the amounts to fit your economy.

- To accomplish the campus mission God has given us we must be fully funded by September 1 — the day students arrive! We still have $845 per month to raise. Will you pray about joining our support team for $100–150 per month?

- You've heard our vision for the $115,000 annex for the homeless, but we cannot reach them alone. Will you pray about a lead gift of $30,000 to $40,000 so we can launch construction April 1?

- Thank you for your faithful support of $15 each month. You have heard about our student mission trip to New Orleans on Spring Break. The students are funding their travel, but by March 30 we will need $12,450 for the discipleship program in the inner city. Will you pray about sponsoring one student for one day — that's $72 or $36 for half a day?

- The conference runs October 12–17 and it costs $535 for each staff. May I ask you to sponsor one or two young staff from West Africa — that's $535 or $1,070? Our deadline is August 15 so they can purchase tickets.

- As Regional Director I am launching the Minnesota Discipleship Fund — total $24,800:

  - Help new staff get established in their unpredictable first year — $12,500

  - Emergencies — $5,400 (we flew a missionary home from Chad last year because of hepatitis)

  - Shepherding young staff families — $2,200 (I travel to each campus twice a year and sometimes I send the staff to professional growth events)

  - Meetings for 525 'outpost' leaders in Minnesota's small towns — $4,700 (these laborers feel cared for when I fund their meetings and provide special discipling materials). May I ask you to pray about a special gift in the $1,000–2,500 range? Our deadline is August 15, our first 'outpost' meeting in Albert Lea.

Like Moses, give your partners specific opportunities to help them feel they can make a difference.

TAKEAWAY

- If someone asked you right now, "What can I do to help support your mission?" what would you say?

- What exact words do you say in appeals? Can they be improved?

- Do the amounts or ranges you suggest have a basis?

- Do you suspect that your staff are not asking specifically? What can you do to help them?

- Are your staff telling the truth to potential partners?

Face-to-Face Fundraising Won't Work

FOR YEARS MISSION LEADERS AROUND THE world told me, "Face to face fundraising appeals *won't work* in my culture." Because this criticism issued from so many cultures, I suspected it *would* work in any culture. Now, after years of teaching around the world, the conclusion is unanimous: When gospel workers respectfully invite friends and acquaintances face to face to join their ministry as giving partners, they say yes.

Face to face communication is powerful. Perhaps you have seen this classic diagram from the Harvard Business Review.

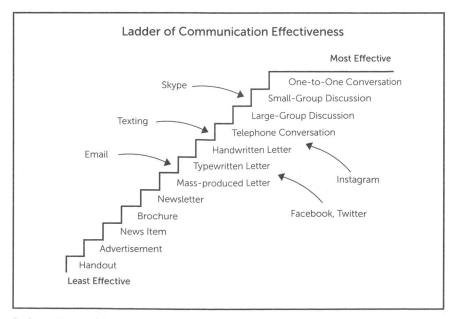

By Scott Morton / Originally Harvard Business Review

I have added social media examples, but one to one conversations are still on top. As a leader don't lose track of JTTTP — *Just Talk To The Person* — both in fundraising and staff communication.

What if one of your staff says, "Face to face appeals don't work. I tried it!" Before you answer, probe for details. Find out how many appeals they made — one-two-ten? Here are questions I ask.

"When you tried face to face appeals for monthly support, did you..."

- Give your prospective partner a commitment card?

- Give a deadline?

- Have this person on your mailing list before the appointment? Has there been any cultivation?

- Explain the agenda when you set the appointment — that you hoped to explain your ministry and funding?

- Sit down for an unhurried conversation? Or was the appeal a few hurried words in the church lobby?

- Share your spiritual journey? Did your prospective giving partner share hers? This is a deeply bonding experience.

- Express passion about your mission?

- Talk more than half the time? Dialogue or monologue?

- Make a clear appeal for *ongoing support*? Exactly what words did you use? Role play what happened.

- Meet with *both* husband and wife?

In my experience with many cultures, workers who "tried" face-to-face without success would answer "No" to some of the questions above. And sometimes more than one face to face encounter is required before a donor will say yes.

I am not suggesting your staff member is poorly funded because of skills mistakes *only*, but start there. If their skills are good, you can look for other issues.

Do not give up on the power of face to face. Did you ask your wife to marry you in a text? Even the Apostle John was unwilling to share "many things" in pen and ink. He said: "...but I hope to see you shortly, and we will speak *face-to-face*" (3 John 14 — italics mine).

But here's a problem: If sending ongoing monthly or quarterly support to a centralized headquarters is unknown in your culture, you will receive discouraging pushback. You will need to educate your culture about ongoing giving for missions. Can it be done?

PRINCIPLE:
In their fundraising and leadership, wise leaders capitalize on the power of face to face communication.

For perspective, the 'deputized method' of monthly support for gospel workers was at one time unknown. It did not become popular in America until after World War II when Cru, Navigators, and Young Life experimented with it in California. Anglo Evangelical culture in America *learned* to give in this way. Your culture can learn it too.

Is it presumptuous to introduce a new way of giving? After all, your culture has timeworn methods of generosity. Why not merge into those giving patterns — like the Harambee of East Africa?

In East Africa when someone gets married or a family member dies, friends gather for a Harambee to support (with cash) the newly married couple or the bereaved — a wonderful generous tradition. But it is *one-time* support.

Similarly, New Testament Greece had a traditional method of charity called *eranoi*. When someone suffered a disaster, the leading citizens gathered a collection. But it was a loan, not a gift.

Also, wealthy patrons funded itinerant Greek philosophers and public works such as aqueducts — they even had their names inscribed on them. All this was accepted by Greek culture.

But Paul taught a radical new *way* to give and a new *reason* to give. He exhorted the new believers to put aside and save "on the first day of every week so that no collections be made when I come" (1 Corinthians 16:2). Money was to be set aside regularly on payday, but not for local emergencies. It was to be sent 500 miles east for the "apostle's church" back in Jerusalem.

Every person and every culture on earth has a giving impulse put there by God since we are created in His likeness. Like Paul, build on that impulse by introducing a new way of giving to your culture — a way that helps you advance the gospel. Be creative, but don't minimize the effectiveness of face to face fundraising for ongoing support. Find a way to make it work in your culture. Like Paul, teach your culture to give in biblical ways.

Teaching giving partners how to give in new ongoing ways has to start somewhere. Let it begin with you!

TAKEAWAY

- What can you do to help your team succeed in face to face fundraising?

- If face to face appeals have not worked in the past, why not? Talk to the donors who said no. Don't rely on your own opinion.

- In what small ways can you begin to teach your culture a new view of giving ongoing monthly or annual support? How about sitting down one on one or with a small group of potential partners using the Bible study in "Appendix B: Creating Your Personal Giving Plan." What a great learning environment you can develop!

Where's Your Titus?

ONE MARK OF SUCCESSFUL LEADERS? THEY deliberately mentor younger leaders. When you receive your job review, you will be asked, "What leaders are you developing? Who is your replacement?" 2 Timothy 2:2 (NIV) says it best:

> *And the things you have heard me say in the presence of many witnesses entrust to reliable people who will also be qualified to teach others.*

Four spiritual generations are pictured — Paul to Timothy to faithful witnesses and finally, to others also. Dawson Trotman, Founder of The Navigators, famously asked, "Where's your man? Where's your woman?"

But today I see experienced leaders traveling *without* younger mentees accompanying them.

Let's take it one step further. Do leaders today take mentees with them on fundraising or donor ministry calls? Have you ever been invited to join a leader on a funding appointment? Have you ever invited someone to join you?

We can learn from Paul. Not only did Paul mentor Timothy, but also Titus! I have pieced together the mysterious narrative of Titus and Paul's fundraising adventures in troublesome Corinth.

The story begins in Ephesus, 200 miles east across the Aegean Sea from Corinth. Paul is dictating 1 Corinthians. In chapter 16:1-4 he exhorts the newly converted Corinthians to give toward "The Collection" for the Apostles in Jerusalem by setting "aside and saving on the first day of every week."

Titus had "made a beginning" in following up on Paul's appeal (2 Corinthians 8:6) but the Corinthians had not actually given even though they were "the first to begin a year ago not only to do this but to desire to do it (2 Corinthians 8:10). And now 12 months has passed. The Corinthians still have not given. (Does this sound familiar?)

Why didn't they follow through? Perhaps because of the problems Paul addressed in 1 Corinthians; party spirit, sexual promiscuity, and eating meat offered to idols, to name three. Besides that, 'super-apostles' had converged on Corinth, and they discredited Paul. More confusion.

Desperate not to lose these converts, Paul made an emergency trip to Corinth to resolve the controversy (13:1 "This is the third time I am coming to you" — not recorded in Acts). Then he sent the famous "severe letter" ("For though I caused you sorrow by my letter..." 7:8). But neither trip nor letter seemed to help.

Was The Collection project dead? Had it been me, I would have let it go. But not Paul. Instead, he asked Titus to travel to Corinth to follow up the funding appeal. A difficult assignment, but Titus was ready:

> For he [Titus] not only accepted our appeal, but being himself very earnest, he has gone to you of his own accord. (2 Corinthians 8:17, emphasis mine)

Of his own accord! Titus wanted to dive into this mess! Leaving Paul in Ephesus, Titus strikes out boldly for Corinth.

The Scriptures don't tell us what Titus did at Corinth, but the Corinthians agreed to follow through on The Collection and make their gift when Paul and the "brothers" arrived (2 Corinthians 9:5). Hooray for Titus!

Titus then departed Corinth heading north to meet Paul who had departed Ephesus traveling west. Getting as far as Troas, Paul had "no rest in his spirit" (2 Corinthians 2:13) so anxious was he to hear from Titus.

Finally they met in Macedonia (probably Philippi) where Titus gave Paul the good news that the Corinthians still respected him and would follow through on The Collection. Paul was overjoyed (2 Corinthians 7:7).

From Macedonia, Paul now confidently writes 2 Corinthians 8–9, his famous giving chapters, made possible because of Titus.

What's the point? Two points actually:

> **PRINCIPLE:**
> Wise leaders mentor future leaders in fundraising by involving them in live bullet funding challenges.

1. When the Corinthians delayed to give what they promised, Paul did not "let it go."

2. He involved his mentee, Titus, in the process of fundraising.

If you hope to fully develop younger leaders, like Paul, take them with you on donor visits and when you speak to your staff about fundraising — the "with him" principle (Mark 3:14). Even consider taking an "office staff" with you. That will bond office and field staff like nothing else.

Bringing next generation leaders alongside you in fundraising is an excellent developmental tactic. Why?

- They will observe your genuine convictions about fundraising — that it is not an "add on" to your leadership.

- They will see you under pressure. This is not dress rehearsal!

- You will learn a ton about them (as they are under pressure), and they will become more vulnerable to share their lives with you. Bonding for life.

I was encouraged last week when I received news from a meeting in Africa. The group was discussing a curriculum for leadership training. They were about to dismiss when Q said, "What about adding fundraising training?" The facilitator, eager to finish said, "It's included under stewardship."

"Not adequate!" said Q. "Fundraising training will be lost unless it stands alone." The group debated and eagerly agreed to add biblical fundraising to the curriculum for leadership training.

Q was a young leader with whom I spent hours in Bible study and coaching over fundraising — he *caught* it. I renamed him Titus!

What can leadership accomplish? A poem by Will Allen Dromgoole (d. 1934).

> *An old man going a lone highway*
> *came at the evening, cold and gray,*
> *To a chasm vast and wide and steep,*
> *with waters rolling cold and deep.*
>
> *The old man crossed in the twilight dim,*
> *the sullen stream had no fears for him;*
> *But he turned when safe on the other side,*
> *and built a bridge to span the tide.*
>
> *"Old man," said a fellow pilgrim near,*
> *"You are wasting your strength with building here.*
> *Your journey will end with the ending day,*
> *you never again will pass this way.*
> *You've crossed the chasm, deep and wide,*
> *Why build you this bridge at eventide?"*
>
> *The builder lifted his old gray head.*
> *"Good friend, in the path I have come," he said,*
> *"There followeth after me today*
> *a youth whose feet must pass this way.*
> *The chasm that was as naught to me,*
> *to that fair-haired youth may a pitfall be;*
> *He, too, must cross in the twilight dim —*
> *Good friend, I am building this bridge for him."*

TAKEAWAY:

- Who are 4–6 younger leaders (like Titus) you are mentoring? What can you do to develop them in biblical fundraising?

- Have you done Bible studies in biblical fundraising with your protégés? Go to scottmorton.net with them to watch and discuss funding topics presented in 3 minute videos.

- Ask your staff this question: "Do you have donors who promised to give but have not followed through? Are you 'just letting it go?' How would Paul advise you?"

Your Organization: Blind Spots In Your Organizational Structure and Systems

Sometimes, and maybe often, organizational practices and policies become bottlenecks for giving. For example:

- *Is your organization set up for online giving?*
- *Do your receipts include a 'turnaround' form for the next gift?*
- *Do you have a 100 percent full funding requirement for field staff?*

"But all things must be done properly and in an orderly manner." (1 Corinthians 14:40).

Organizational procedures are just as spiritual as your heartfelt prayed over sermons and speeches. Your administrative practices reflect who you are as an organization. Donors notice if things are done well or poorly, including accuracy of math, timeliness of receipting, clarity of graphics, even spelling.

Lack of trust or cooperation between departments is another organizational blindspot that can wreak havoc on a ministry's effectiveness and integrity with donors.

Wherever you are in the organizational ladder you must not ignore the lurking dangers of organizational blind spots. They will eventually impede field staff funding and donors' enthusiasm. Speak up before it is too late.

Do Your Systems Make Giving Difficult?

IS IT EASY TO GIVE TO your organization? Before you answer, put yourself in the shoes of a non-donor. Go to your organization's website or review your organizational brochure.

- Can you *easily* find the *Give* or *Donate* button? How many clicks to complete a gift? Does your brochure *clearly* explain how to give?

- Can you easily *designate* your gift for a staff or project?

- Monthly giving — can you set up a standing electronic bank order or a recurring credit card order *without human interaction*?

- Can you find instructions about stock gifts or gifts-in-kind? What about legacy giving through a will?

We are so familiar with our procedures and lingo that we forget how strange our *simple* instructions sound to newcomers. If your potential giving partners struggle with the logistical details of sending a gift, they will put if off until later — which means never!

King Joash made giving uncomplicated. After his Levites failed to collect Moses' half shekel, he simply bored a hole in a chest and set it beside the gate. Passersby could easily give. Similarly, the Apostle Paul made giving simple. He traveled to Corinth to pick up the gifts personally.

Last week we received a letter from a mission-

PRINCIPLE:

Leaders ensure that giving is made uncomplicated for giving partners. Giving logistics must not deter givers.

ary friend asking for support, but he included no commitment card, no return envelope and no website address. We wanted to give, but we had to search for the organization's physical address and find our own envelope. Those neglected details made us think twice about the credibility of the organization.

In developing countries this is a big headache. If the postal or banking infrastructure is undependable, your giving partners will postpone making giving decisions. Even more if they have to travel across town to search for your office and hand cash to a clerk.

Like Joash, use creativity to solve this problem! Don't force donors and your staff to come up with workarounds. Here is what I have seen creative National Directors do in developing countries where the infrastructure is undependable:

- Get the facts. What exactly are the logistical holdups? Talk with staff, banks, post offices, even donors. A problem well defined is half solved.

- Win the cooperation of one or two banks. Ask them to creatively help your donors channel their gifts to your national account and secondly to designated staff accounts — without extra fees.

- Hire a dependable courier on a fast motorbike to collect gifts all over town.

- If banks can't direct gifts to staff, ask the donors to give an odd amount. For example, 501.5 Naira is for Edwin's support, 501.7 Naira is for VJ, and so on.

- Train your office staff with a customer service spirit to work winsomely with donors who bring cash. Ensure the donors leave the office blessed and with a plan for making it easier next month. Invite them to give monthly. Give a small gift, like a spiritual help booklet to first-time givers.

By making it easy to give, you are helping your giving partners become faithful disciples.

TAKEAWAY

- What logistical obstacles must your donors overcome to give to your organization?

- Are your field staff's instructions to donors in sync with those given by your office staff?

- Do your appeal letters include a return envelope and an easy to understand commitment card with account numbers?

- Do your pledge cards have your organizational address, phone number, email address, website address, and clear directions on giving?

- Can donors give online easily? How many clicks to give a gift to a staff?

- Is your website mobile friendly?

- Can your staff email potential donors a direct link to their personal online giving page?

- Receipting and office:

  - How long does it take for givers to get an acknowledgement of their gift? Aim for 48–72 hours.

  - Do the receipts include a turnaround slip and envelope for easily giving the next gift?

  - Does your receipt say thank you and does it have a small story about your work? Is there a signature from the National Director? Is his or her signature readable?

  - Has your office staff been trained in how to treat walk-in and phone-in donors with respect and gratefulness?

  - Do your office staff know how to invite a walk-in donor to sign up for monthly electronic gifts?

- Your website: Try it yourself! Make a small gift for several staff and projects to challenge the system.

- Make a small gift to other organizations to see how they treat donors. What can you learn?

Communications and Receipting Aligned?

YOUR COMMUNICATIONS AND RECEIPTING TEAMS INTERACT daily with giving partners. This is often a donor's first experience with your organization, and it is crucial they are treated well. As CEO you must understand what they do. Because their competency and high morale are crucial to your organization, helping these teams function at high capacity is wise leadership.

Receipting and Communications must be on the same page as your Leadership Group and Development Staff. Your receipting department promotes organizational fundraising values. They must not consider themselves stand alone departments.

Receipting: Is it merely an *administrative minor detail*? No, receipting is an important component of the *funding strategy*. And it starts with *timeliness.*

Young King Joash demonstrated timeliness indirectly. Not only did he set up a chest in front of the gate where Moses' half shekel could be easily given, but he also emptied the chest *daily* (2 Chronicles 24:11–12). The money was given *immediately* to the workmen.

Have you ever sent a gift to an organization and waited weeks to get an acknowledgement? Joash would be appalled.

I urge you to send receipts within 48–72 hours of receiving a gift. Some organizations try to save money by sending receipts quarterly or annually, but donors like to know quickly if you received the gift. If it comes ninety days or a year later they assume you are inept. Prompt gift acknowledgement communicates that your ministry is well run. Also, the sooner donors receive acknowledgements, the sooner they can send another gift. Like Joash, "empty the chest" daily.

When problems come up (and they will), train a few receipting staff to interact with dissatisfied donors. Although your receipting team might be excellent at receipting details, they might not be good at customer service, even if they have been 'trained.' Detailed workers often don't mind telling donors where the donors are wrong. Be careful about who is assigned to customer service.

Communications, here is a simple guideline: Your communications strategy must be in sync with your organizational fundraising strategy. This helps avoid confusing your branding in the public eye.

In saying Communications and Receipting must align with your fundraising strategy, I assume Leadership and Development are properly aligned. Are they?

Where to start with your Communications and Receipting teams? Two long lunches — one with Receipting and another with Communications. Ask them to prepare answers to these questions with samples:

Receipting Team:

- Show me our "new donor welcome package"? Don't have one? Oops.

- Is our gift receipt form graphically pleasing and easy to understand? Is a next gift form and envelope included so donors can easily give again? Is online giving explained?

- Do receipts include a warm thank you from the CEO?

- How many days from the time a gift arrives until the receipt is sent? More than three days? Oops!

- What complaints are we hearing from donors? Are these complaints being passed along to decision makers so improvements can be made?

- What procedure do we employ when we make errors? Do we have gifted customer service team members connecting with donors? Suggestion: phoning immediately communicates care.

- Are donors offered standing bank orders, electronic funds transfers, or recurring credit card giving? Is human intervention needed?

- How is the relationship between Field Staff, Development, Receipting, and Communications?

Communications Team:

- What information do donors receive from us besides their receipt? How often do they hear from us? Do they only hear from us when we need funding?

- Does our communication with donors support the fundraising strategy?

- Are the receipt copy and communication pieces in sync with organizational branding and the strategy of the CEO?

- Our website: How many clicks to make a designated gift?

- Is the language in our communications understandable to readers? Do we use in-house lingo? Are we telling stories?

- Do our writers seek to 'create an image' (nonsense!) or do their articles compel readers to take action?

- Do our communications include stories from satisfied donors on why they give? Are we teaching about biblical giving? (Don't shy away from money in your communications strategy.)

Your receipting and communications teams have an often thankless job. Show appreciation by explaining how they are an important part of the team. Ask them how the organization can be improved. Because they are in touch with donors, they will have valuable ideas.

TAKEAWAY

- Identify two or three items from the lists above to improve your communications and receipting ministries.

- Do your receipting people realize how important they are in connecting with donors? How can you explain that to them?

- To solve alignment problems, have you considered having your Receipting and Communications teams report to Development?

- When donors contact your organization, who takes the call? Are they well trained in customer service?

- Read one of your communication pieces aloud to a family member. Did it inspire him or her?

Objectively Evaluating Your Development Team

SO HOW WILL YOU MEASURE SUCCESS in your development function? As the old joke goes: "Development's mission statement has only one word — *More!*" Ha ha!

To lead well in the complicated world of corporate fundraising, use the Five Pillars below as an easy to remember mental model.

Essential Pillars of Corporate Funding

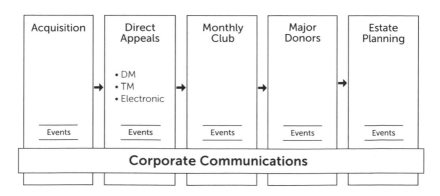

The five pillars are generally sequential. For example:

- A donor gives her first gift — *acquisition.*

- Next she receives *direct appeals* for subsequent gifts.

- Thirdly, she is invited to a *monthly club* (steady cash flow).

- Next, the major donor team determines if she is capable of a *major gift.* If yes, they phone or visit her.

- Over time, she is invited to include your ministry in her *estate plans*.

Corporate Communications weaves into the Development Pillars but should be driven by the fundraising strategy. Communications is not a stand alone department.

Yes, this chart is oversimplified, but do you see the progression? From a meager first gift to becoming such a good friend that she includes your organization in her estate plans. D-e-v-e-l-o-p-m-e-n-t!

Events can be included in each pillar. For example:

- Open House at your facility to invite first gifts.

- Get acquainted breakfast with new donors. Invite them to join the monthly club.

- Club member desserts to meet local staff.

- Major donor funding banquet.

- President's Weekend to minister to top donors.

- Estate planning luncheons for selected older donors.

Note: Events take time. If your overworked clerical team adds events to their jobs, morale suffers (even though they might still be smiling). You need an event planner — perhaps temporarily.

Leaders Must Know the Development Process

As CEO you must understand the development process and you must build a collegial trusting relationship with your development team.

Here's your assignment: invite your development team for two long lunches. If you don't have a development team, do this exercise with your accounting or administration staff.

For the first lunch take the Pillars Chart with you. Lay it on the table and start with two questions:

1. Help me understand what "we" do in each pillar.

2. Give me examples of how the pillars are working together or are not working together.

Your task at this first lunch is to listen and win hearts. Resist the CEO tendency to pontificate. Ask clarification questions only. Let the development team teach you what they actually do. You'll see huge gaps that need attention. Relax.

Now you are ready for your next lunch. Ask the development team to prepare answers to the following questions using the Pillars Chart as your outline.

Thirteen Strategic Questions to Ask Development

Acquisition:

1. How many new donors are we acquiring annually? What prompts first gifts?

2. What is our gross cost to acquire a new donor? (Note: The cost of acquiring will be higher than their gift. Don't panic. Smile and keep eating your Caesar salad.)

Direct Mail/Telephone/Electronic Appeals:

3. How many pieces of direct mail go out each year? Phone appeals? E-mail appeals? Social media appeals?

4. Response rates for each appeal? (Warning — it is in single digits! Don't choke on your Chicken Parmigiana.) Average gift of each?

5. How do current response rates and average gifts compare with previous years?

6. How many times a year do we ask? Be ready for an "audience-segmentation" answer.

7. What is our retention rate of new donors in their second year? Third year? (Be prepared for jaw dropping disappointment. Loosen your tie.)

Monthly Club:

8. How many members? How are we growing the club? Average gift increasing?

Major Donors:

9. Are qualified major donor prospects being culled from the first three pillars and handed to the major donor team? Action plan for these new leads?

10. Who are the 50 largest current donors to our organization? Is there a development appeal plan for each one? Which ones are you assigning to me?

11. Is the major donor team getting adequate cooperation from me? From other national and regional leaders?

PRINCIPLE:

Organizational leaders must embrace their fundraising responsibilities by understanding the development process and building mutual trust and cooperation with their Development Team.

Estate Planning:

12. Are we keeping accurate records of those with whom we have estate agreements (contracts)? How are we cultivating them?

13. What is the marketing plan to add more agreements?

Working with the Team:

Building teamwork and trust with Development is not optional. Here are some benchmarks and ideas:

- Is your Development Director (or gifted money person) a voting member of your leadership team? He or she should be.

- Has Development given you ten to twenty major donors for whom you are the primary cultivator — your portfolio?

- Do you have *unhurried* quarterly meetings with your development team to review major donors *name by name*? Agenda (ask these questions):

- What are you doing with each donor in your portfolio?

- Who are you seeing next?

- For what project? How much will you ask?

- When will you see them?

- Is a national leader going with you?

- Does your development team feel jazzed about the vision of the organization?

- Do you have confidence in your development team?

Caution: CEO, you have power, but learn to appreciate the knowledge, skills, and experience of your development team. Development will try to obey your directives even when you are wrong. If you are unhappy with your development team, talk to them before you complain to others.

Return on Investment

Here's another benchmark to use with the five pillars: return on investment (ROI) of each pillar. The ROIs shown reflect only actual costs of fundraising activities and are based on my experience in America. They do not include fixed costs like salaries, utilities, benefits, office equipment, etc.

Acquisition: *.5 to 1.0 ROI (for a dollar spent you'll receive 50 cents to $1.00 in return)*

Acquisition often loses money. Don't insist on it making a profit.

Direct Appeals: *2.0 to 4.0 ($2–4 received for a dollar spent)*

If your goal is to increase the donor base you can settle for lower ROIs like 2.0 to 2.5. But if you seek net income, aim at 3.0 to 4.0. Phone appeals at 1.5 are acceptable because phone calls recruit lapsed donors better than direct mail.

Monthly Club: 6.0 to 8.0

Dependable cash flow! Encourage club members to give monthly through their banks, credit cards, or phones.

Major Donors: 3.0 to 10.0

Higher during capital campaigns. For example, visiting a donor twice may cost $2,500 (air ticket, rental car, hotel) but could result in a $25,000 gift — a 10:1 ROI.

Estate Planning: 1.0 to huge

For current cash this pillar is fortunate to break even. Donors often give much more in their estate than in current cash. Inform your entire donor base that estate gifts can be given. It is not only major donors who give through estates, but smaller givers are good prospects if they have given frequently.

TAKEAWAY

- As CEO, is fundraising/donor ministry one of your top three or four priorities?
- Do you and your development team meet at least quarterly?
- Has Development given you a portfolio of major donors you are expected to cultivate and ask?
- Do you join development team members on funding appeals or donor ministry calls?
- Do you keep Development informed about organizational news, strategy and personnel changes?
- Do you invite your development team to teach you about fundraising?
- Do you joyfully embrace your fundraising role as CEO?
- Do you speak well of fundraising or do you telegraph funding is a necessary evil?

Are Development and
Leadership on the Same Page?

MY CEO FRIEND, YOU MAY NOT like this quote, but it is absolutely true.

"I've rarely encountered an institutional leader who has had the patience, the time, or the experience to permit him or her to truly appreciate the dynamics of the professional development operation."[8]

In large organizations, conflicts between CEOs and development departments are legendary. The money guys think national leaders should give forty percent of their time to fundraising, as if they had nothing else to do! Development people have a knack for loading guilt onto leaders whose consciences are already overworked.

At the same time, national leaders look suspiciously at Development. Why can't they deliver more money — and faster?

My CEO friend, you might know plenty about fundraising, but you don't know as much as your veteran development team. Humble yourself to learn to think like the development guys. Ask them what you should do. Their morale will skyrocket!

King Joash had a conflict with his development team, the Levites. To rebuild the temple, Joash delegated fundraising to the Levites (his full-time staff), telling them to gather the money quickly. But they did not perform quickly enough, so he sacked them.

2 Kings 12:1–16 adds an important detail. The money collected by the Levites was *commingled* — sacred offerings, personal vows, and voluntary gifts — all mixed together. The priests failed to separate the temple repair money from other gifts so the repair cash was "lost."

Wisely, Joash instructed the priests to "Take no more money from your treasurers, but hand it over for repairing the temple" (2 Kings 12:7 NIV). Joash's top priority was repairing the temple, but the Levites were not on the same page as their king.

That is a problem still today. Do you and your funding team have the same priorities? A COO friend recently told me that their organization lost several major donors because their fundraising guy was at odds with what the President was teaching.

PRINCIPLE:
The CEO and leadership teams must be aligned with their development teams on funding priorities and values, while building mutual trust and cooperation.

Before jumping on the fundraisers for not being aligned, ask yourself if you have been clear in communicating organizational priorities. Has your leadership trumpet given "an uncertain sound?"

For if the trumpet gives an uncertain sound, who shall prepare himself to the battle? (1 Corinthians 14:8 KJV)

You may think you have been consistent, but ask around. I find that busy top leaders sometimes give mixed signals to their fundraising teams depending on the pressures coming across their desk. For example, a CEO told a development team to focus on international projects, but two weeks later he switched to domestic projects because of the immediate cash flow pressure he faced. Because he was under pressure, he didn't realize his instructions were contradictory.

It is not what you *think* you said that matters. What do others actually hear?

And of course, funding priorities do change when tragedies strike. Keep good communications with your money team so they can keep up with you.

For fundraisers I have this question: What are you doing to ensure you can passionately represent your CEO or your regional director's priorities? Why not initiate conversations with your leaders about their priorities rather than piously expecting them to come to you?

Don't put the burden of communication on them. You take the initiative. Be more humble. Buy them lunch.

Both you and the CEO must agree that the CEO's fundraising capacity is an important tool in your organizational funding toolbox. Be wise in what you ask the CEO to do. Work together with the CEO to determine where his or her help is most strategic. It may change from time to time. Teamwork!

CEO, please understand that your most urgent funding priorities are often not attractive to donors. For example, $15,000 for an urgently needed HR meeting might be high on your list, but it will not motivate donors. Your development guy will explain that to you. Be patient. Have a range of giving opportunities to present to major donors.

There's another practical lesson here from Joash. Distribute gifts according to the donor's wishes — no commingling. Resist pressure from those who need the money. You must obey donor intent.

TAKEAWAY

- Are you and your development team on the same page?
- What can you do to ensure they understand your priorities?
- Have you and Development worked out a portfolio of 10–20 top donors for you to manage and appeal to?
- Development people: Are you initiating communication? Are you learning to trust your leaders?

One-Person Fundraising
Departments—Don't Quit!

AS A ONE-PERSON DEVELOPMENT DEPARTMENT FOR your organization, you do not have internal comrades to "talk fundraising" with you. The leaders of your ministry might try to encourage you in your fundraising role, but they speak from a different clan. Their *tribal smell* is not familiar. They're sincere, but they don't get it.

Here's more troubling news: The life span of development officers (like you) is only two years before they move on. Sorry. One common reason they move on is because their leaders expect them to raise unrealistic amounts of money "by next month." Just six weeks ago a friend of mine was sacked after seven months on the job because he was not bringing in money fast enough!

Even though your boss understands intellectually that it takes months and even years to cultivate big gifts, he or she is under pressure to fund the organization — and you are being paid handsomely, but have not yet brought in much income to offset your expense. But don't feel any pressure!

This means you must develop good relationships with your bosses, and you must also "teach up" — help your leaders understand the fundraising process like you do.

Do three things.

1. Take initiative to find biblical fundraising encouragement and professional growth. Build your own fundraising mini-culture so you are not alone — and find a coach.

You can't help others if you are dying inside. Ideas:

- Once a year attend a professional fundraising seminar like Christian Leadership Association or Support Raising Solutions Training (SupportRaisingSolutions.org). Go online for podcasts if you can't attend in person.

- Find a mentor or at least a fundraising peer. Even if he or she is across the country or from a different country, find someone with whom you can share your heart and your questions once a month — in person or on Skype. You could:

  - Read this book together and discuss it.

  - Do funding Bible studies (scottmorton.net has downloadable studies and 3 minute videos to discuss).

  - Discuss one Bible passage on funding each time you meet.

  - Talk through your "department strategy" starting with your official mission, goals, and action steps.

  - Accompany one another on funding appointments (if you are able to visit in person).

- Devote two hours per week to personal Bible study on fundraising. Let God speak to you.

- Devote two hours weekly to read about fundraising and donor ministry.

- Subscribe to the *NonProfit Times* and *MovieMondays.com.*

- Start a fundraising library. Collect the best books, articles, and electronic clips.

- Start an informal gathering of local fundraising colleagues.

  - Pray together.

  - Ask someone to teach a topic at each meeting.

- Show one another your website and organizational literature (sparks ideas).

- Study a funding scripture together.

2. Follow the suggestions in Chapter 33 on development and leadership teamwork. Seek to influence but also directly teach your leaders and peers about the ministry of fundraising. Share scriptures, war stories, and statistics to help them adopt your values.

PRINCIPLE:

One person development departments must 'teach up' to educate leaders about the fundraising process, and they must work hard to find fundraising mentors and encouragement.

3. Take your leaders on fundraising or donor ministry appointments. Accompany them too. As they see what you do they will copy it. As you see what they do, you can offer suggestions.

Don't give up. Go back to your calling and your life scripture verse(s). Your depth with the Lord will sustain you. If God has led you here, now is not the time to wallow in self pity. Resist the temptation to be busy, busy, busy. You cannot meet every demand coming your way, nor get all your work done by the end of every day. You can always call one more person or write one more letter. A fundraiser's work is never finished.

Therefore, you must take time to feed yourself in biblical fundraising, because others within your organization cannot.

TAKEAWAY

- From the bullet list in #1 above, what can you put into immediate action?

- Whom can you invite to be a Skype partner once a month to talk about biblical funding?

- What immediate actions can you take to influence your boss and peers in biblical funding?

Fundraisers and Leaders Must Close
the Understanding/Trust Gap

BECAUSE I SERVED TWENTY-SIX YEARS ON a national development team (thirteen as vice president) this chapter is a no-crapola-gutsy talk to the development family. Fasten your seat belt.

I agree with Berendt and Taft, who point out:

> *"[There's an]* **understanding gap** *between chief executives and development officers…a problem that produces turnover, waste, and inefficiency."*[9] *(emphasis mine)*

Understanding gap is understated. Misunderstandings soon evolve into we/they silos of mistrust with each party protecting turf. The result is an uneasy peace between leadership and the fundraisers with suspicion on both sides. Here are five recommendations for development staff to help close the *understanding/trust gap* — and you may not like them!

- *Take initiative to develop trusting relationships with your leaders.*

   When I say, "take initiative," I mean pick up the phone. I hear you saying, "If the President wants to talk, he *should* call me!" Maybe he *should* call you, but I'm telling you he *won't* call you. You are merely one of nineteen prairie fires he is throwing water on this week. That big issue you brought to him 10 days ago? He forgot about it 20 minutes after you left his office. Stop giving yourself permission to sulk.

   Love takes initiative. Be the first to break the ice so you can work together in a trusting, loving, even enjoyable way. Did I say *loving*?

Yes. As *Christians* we are expected to love one another, not just figure out how to survive in a win/lose toxic environment. Jesus expects nothing less:

But love your enemies, and do good, and lend, expecting nothing in return... (Luke 6:35)

PRINCIPLE:

As a development staff, it is your responsibility to develop loving and productive working relationships with organizational leaders in authority over you.

Your leaders are not your enemies — or are they? Take initiative to love them, do good to them, and expect nothing in return. Then you can weather any misunderstanding.

I often said to our development staff, "I can't explain why Field Director 'Bob' made that 'anti-fundraising' decision, but I do know you must love him. It is not your job to 'figure him out.' It is your job to love him. I expect nothing less of you."

- *Humbly and creatively educate leadership about development.*

What is accomplished by constantly complaining *the leaders don't get it!* Instead of whining, teach them about fundraising, realizing you have plenty to learn too.

Development people say, "But I don't have *authority* to teach my superiors!" Yada yada yada. Development people are rarely (maybe never) given organizational authority. If you need authority to do your job you will fail anyway. Win their trust and guide them through your *influence*. Use *personal* authority rather than *positional* authority.

How to influence your leaders? Try this:

- *Modeling:* Tell about a recent fundraising encounter and how God showed up.

- *Scripture:* Share how scriptures on funding help you in your job.

- *Take them with you on appointments:* As they see what you do, they will learn, even if the appointments don't go well.

- *Go with them on their appointments:* After an appointment or two, ask, "What did we do well on that appointment?" Give at least one compliment then ask, "What could we have done better?"

- Next, "How did *I* do? Anything *I* missed today?" Graciously accept what he/she tells you.

- If your leader asks for critique, don't unload 17 criticisms. Share a couple suggestions with specific examples of what he/she did well and poorly. Unless you illustrate specifics, your leader will feel attacked.

- *Professional development:* Ask to lead brief professional growth modules for leadership team meetings. Include scriptures.

- *Think like your leaders think.*

Remove your fundraising hat and put on the CEO or the regional leader's hat. When they notice that you address issues from *their* perspective, they will appreciate you more. You need more than one string on your banjo.

- *Bring solutions, not problems.*

I recently saw an advertisement with a CEO in front of her desk pleading, "Problems I got! Bring me solutions!"

Rather than whining that a leader won't make her fundraising appointments, ask her, "How can I help you get these appointments?" For example, if funding is weak in Cleveland, don't merely point that out. Present an action plan that includes you meeting her in Cleveland to visit three key donors — and you arrange the appointments.

If your solution requires your leader to *initiate* extensive action, it will fail.

- *Confront when necessary.*

  You will run into differences of opinion, but don't assume you are always wrong. Biblical fundraising must be brought into the mainstream of our organizations, and that means you can't just "let stuff go." Sometimes leaders seriously sin, and sometimes they make innocent mistakes. Either way, you need to lovingly confront or it will happen again.

  But when you confront, be biblical. Gossiping that the "president doesn't get it" is not biblical. Two reminders from Matthew 18:15 (emphasis mine):

  *If your brother sins, go and show him his fault **in private**; if he listens to you, you have won your brother. (Matthew 18:15)*

  In private! The New International Version says, "just between the two of you." In NGO's we talk too much *about* one another instead of talking *to* one another. What will you gain by embarrassing your leaders in public?

  Second, "show him his *fault*" does not mean "cuss him out." Limit your comments to the specific error — the exact fault, detailing time and place and circumstances. If appropriate, connect his error to a trend of missteps that hurt the work, but don't go into his childhood wounding or criticize him for being born in Texas.

  Language like the following helps me be non combative (helpful phrases in bold):

  *George, I truly want to **work together** as your partner. I **wonder if I could share an impression** from our appeals in Cleveland last week.*

  *During our dinner with the Rosen's and the Avila's, **did you notice** Al's reaction when you interrupted him to tell about your kids? Actually, you interrupted twice. [Pause.] Yes, you noticed? You continued talking, but Al didn't say anything the rest of the dinner. **I could be wrong**, but I think he lost interest in the project at that point. **Help me understand** why you kept talking.*

Don't make an issue about *every* leadership mistake. Stop whining! Whining might make you feel better, but it doesn't advance a solution. If you whine but don't confront your leaders, you disqualify yourself from being part of the solution. Call the "Waaahmbulance!"

In which direction do you lean; overly loyal or debate every issue? Ask God to give you the grace to initiate building relationships of trust with your ministry leaders. Lay down your sword.

TAKEAWAY

If you lead a development team, can you answer yes to these questions?

- Do you and your CEO (or supervisor) agree on his/her role in fundraising?

- Do you respect the CEO's time constraints and understand that fundraising is only one of his/her many tasks?

- Do you initiate bimonthly or quarterly update meetings with the CEO, his/her leaders, and your fundraising team? As a service to him/her, do you prepare and lead the agenda? Do you initiate additional private meetings if needed?

- Are you willing to let the CEO teach you about the organization?

- Do you consider the CEO an important member of your fundraising team?

- Do you keep the CEO informed about the status of donors and campaigns?

- Do you do the preparation work necessary to help the CEO succeed in fundraising?

- Issues that you have been brooding over, do you share them selectively with the CEO?

- Do you trust and respect the CEO?

How it worked for me—a confession:
During my years in development, I let too much go. I should have confronted both my leaders and my staff more. I went to bed too many nights with an ache in my soul because I swallowed hard and decided not to rock the boat over goofy decisions from my leaders and lame excuses from my staff. I was overly loyal. I don't blame others; I blame me for not speaking up.

If I could do it over, I would pick fewer battles but confront with more conviction.

Moses helps me. After escaping from Egypt, Moses was sitting dejectedly at a water well in the desert as the daughters of Jethro watered their flocks. Soon male shepherds arrived with their flocks and shoved the women aside. Moses could have let it go like I often did. But Exodus 3:2 says, "Moses stood up" to confront the wrongdoers. Now, like Moses, I have determined to stand up to confront wrongs more quickly—and lovingly!

Maximizing Results From Fundraising Events

SOONER OR LATER YOU WILL BE asked to make an appeal at a fundraising event. But do you know how? It is assumed that ministry leaders are instinctively good at this. Sorry.

Until someone shows you a better plan, here are ten guidelines I've learned the hard way — not only in how to ask, but also how to plan a successful group fundraiser.

1. *Don't surprise the audience.*

   If your attendees do not know in advance that an offering will be taken, you risk a poor response and alienating potential partners. How do you like it when your host pulls out a sales presentation at a neighborhood social?

   You might plead, "They should know we always take offerings." Even if everyone "knows," that is a cavalier attitude. If they are surprised, will they give as generously? Would you?

   If you intend to make an appeal, even a low-key appeal, make that clear in your invitation, not after the guests arrive.

2. *Lower your expectations.*

   Like kids at their first carnival, inexperienced planners pump up expectations for the gazillions they will raise "next Friday night!" However, in my experience 50 percent of the donors in the room give nothing. Even so, they enjoyed the meal and will say good things about you at the office Monday morning.

Of the half who give, 25 percent give exactly what you requested, 25 percent give slightly below, and 50 percent give a token amount, perhaps what they think it cost for the chicken dinner.

Mega-donors do not attend events. Go to them face to face.

3. *Follow-up is essential.*

Once the event is over, the hard work doesn't stop. Send a personalized follow up letter to all attendees announcing the total given. Include a commitment slip for those who did not give and invite them to give at a future time. Remind them of your ministry purpose or re-emphasize a dynamite testimony they heard at the event.

For those who gave, include a grateful acknowledgement of their gift or pledge with instructions on how to complete their giving. For larger gifts, you might also phone to say thanks.

Send a letter to those who were invited but didn't come. Give a glowing report on the evening they 'missed', and include an appeal with a pledge card.

Remember, an event is only one part of your strategy to build a faithful giving partner team — that's why it is called d-e-v-e-l-o-p-m-e-n-t.

4. *Do your homework.*

First, analyze the metrics of previous fundraising events. Are new donors making gifts, or are you getting the same amounts from the same attendees? Is gift size increasing? Don't give yourself high marks merely because, "Everyone had a great time!"

For the upcoming event, answer these questions:

- For what project will you appeal? Project total?

- What do you want each attendee to consider giving? Make a giving pyramid. See "Appendix G: Project Pyramid."

- How will you bring emotion to your presentation? How will you help people visualize what their gifts will do?

- Do you want cash now, a one year pledge, a three year pledge?

- Who will make the appeal? Are they trained to do this? Beware of having celebrities or community leaders who are well known but untrained in asking.

- Commitment card. Will donors know how to give just by looking at it? (Yes, you must use a card. It is your silent reminder in the weeks ahead.)

Don't prepare in a vacuum. Gather your fundraising people with your ministry leaders and a few faithful giving partners. Evaluate the giving capacity of the attendees to help establish your goal in asking.

5. *Keep the actual appeal short and interesting.*

   After the testimonies and explanations of your mission, keep the appeal itself short and interesting — 15 minutes tops. Include teaching on biblical giving. Have a current donor explain in three minutes why they support your work generously — but rehearse with them and time them! We once had a 'testimonial' go 40 minutes. Oops.

6. *Include emotion — speak to hearts.*

   Remember Moses. He appealed to "every man whose heart moves him" (Exodus 25:2).

   Without emotion, your appeal will fall flat. How will you speak to donors' hearts so they can visualize how their giving will make a difference?

   Tell stories hot from the field. Show pictures of people who benefit from your work. Play a three minute video about a field project. Interview someone from the field — a changed life.

At a major donor fundraiser weekend for a military ministry, we invited a soldier newly home from Iraq to speak. He was not polished, but for ten minutes he held the audience spellbound by describing fellow soldiers who wanted to be in Bible study and others who wanted nothing to do with God even though they risked death daily from IEDs. He asked us to pray for his buddies still "over there." There was not a dry eye in the house.

Can you be overly dramatic? Yes. To avoid that smarmy quiz show host demeanor, make sure your stories are absolutely true. Your emotional story doesn't have to be a tearjerker. Simply share how your ministry touches human hearts on the frontlines.

7. *Watch out for "poor talk."*

    Talk about your God-given compelling passion, not your dreary financial needs. Invite people to join your vision, not to bail you out. Here are toxic words to avoid (highlighted):

    - "Our *need* is to repair the library."

    - "Not everyone can give the amounts I've suggested, but *every little bit helps.*"

    - "Maybe God is calling you to be a *prayer partner or a volunteer* instead of giving."

    - "Not everyone *can afford* to give at this level."

    - "Our budgets are minimal. *No one is getting rich in this organization.*" (Why arouse suspicion?)

8. *Rehearse your presentation with a fundraising guru.*

    "Failing to rehearse is rehearsing to fail." Rehearse with a development team staff or funding guru who does *not* have the gift of mercy.

    Rehearsing frees your mind so you can concentrate on your audience. When you are worried about what you'll say next, you cannot give your heart to your listeners.

9. *Pray, pray, pray.*

    Your team will work hard to get people to the event, but there is something they can't do — sovereignly direct God's people to make stewardship decisions.

10. *Teach about biblical giving.*

    Donors need to be reminded that they are stewards, not owners. Ask boldly, but also teach briefly from a Bible passage — not to guilt them into giving — but because giving is part of discipleship.

TAKEAWAY:

- Debrief with your team after the event. Review in light of the Ten Guidelines.

- Of the Ten Guidelines, which two or three must you keep in mind for next time?

- How do funding events fit into your overall funding strategy? Or do they?

Volunteers: To increase attendance and recruit qualified new donors, use volunteers as table hosts (and other responsibilities also). Train them well. An untrained volunteer with a good heart is not nearly as effective as a trained volunteer with a good heart. Without training, their pride in your organization will dissipate. Don't forget to invite them to give.

Business Income or Gift Income?

A CONTROVERSY IS BOILING AMONG MISSIONS leaders today.

Should missions be funded by income from businesses set up in the culture? Or from traditional gift income donors?

The momentum is on the side of business as mission (BAM). A megachurch missions leader recently told me they consider standard "support raising" as passé — out of favor. "It was successful for a time," she said, "but that was for a different generation."

In Chapter 15 the ABFR (anything but fundraising) issue was addressed, but here is additional biblical background you ought to know to help you make wise decisions.

BAM advocates look to the Apostle Paul as their model for mission workers being funded by business tactics. But was tent making Paul's primary method of funding?

During Paul's 20 or so years of ministry, he made tents only three times that we know of, at Thessalonica, Corinth, and Ephesus.

Thessalonica

Paul, the Jewish church planter, determined "not to be a [financial] burden" to the newly converted Greek believers (1 Thessalonians 2:9). If he had taken money from them they might assume he was a charlatan like other wandering philosophers.

Later he modeled manual labor for certain lazy Thessalonians who lived off church funds because they thought Christ was returning soon (2 Thessalonians 3:7–15).

Corinth

Paul made tents with Aquila and Priscilla but stopped when Silas and Timothy arrived from Macedonia with money (Acts 18:1–5). Most scholars believe he never went back to tent making at Corinth. He would not accept Corinthian funding so as to contrast himself from false teachers, even showing a hint of sarcasm:

> For in what respect were you treated as inferior to the rest of the churches, except that I myself did not become a [financial] burden to you? Forgive me this wrong! (2 Corinthians 12:13, emphasis mine)

However, after leaving Corinth, Paul received at least one gift (at Ephesus) from the Corinthian household of Stephanas, the first converts in Achaia who "had devoted themselves for ministry to the saints" (1 Corinthians 16:15-17). Interesting.

Ephesus

Scholars are not sure why Paul made tents during his nearly three years in Ephesus.

> You yourselves know that these hands ministered to my own needs and to the men who were with me. (Acts 20:34)

Perhaps he did not seek gift income because of the silversmith controversy (Acts 19:23–41). The silversmith Demetrius fomented a riot because Paul's preaching discouraged customers from buying silver shrines of the Goddess Diana. Paul was bad for Demetrius's business. Paul's decision to support himself eroded Demetrius's claim that Paul was a money-grabber.

Again, interestingly, when Paul left Ephesus the Ephesians gave for his journey to Judea (Acts 20:38 propempo).

Before you decide between BAM or gift income funding, a worldwide misnomer — *the sacred-secular misunderstanding* — must be resolved. Let me explain.

The historic lay/cleric separation unfortunately repeats the lie that only clerics do ministry while laypeople fund them. Even though all believers are *full time*, mission history shows laypeople have been marginalized in favor of *full time* workers. But biblically, one is not more important than the other.

Years ago pioneer missions leader LeRoy Eims introduced himself to a conference attender. The conferee gave his name and where he was from. Then he added, "I'm just a layman."

Eims flinched! "Just a layman! Just a layman!" Eims exclaimed. "You're not just a layman. You are the key to reaching the world!"

If laypeople are the key, then what is the value of gift income workers?

May I share a personal story illustrating the unintended consequences of *not* having full time workers?

In my 20s, I worked for a local newspaper in Missouri. At the same time I was launching a ministry among college students. I was doing well in my newspaper job, and simultaneously on campus. Students were coming to Christ and growing in discipleship. God was blessing me in both business and campus ministry.

But I was burning out. I worked long hours at the newspaper and spent many late nights on campus shepherding a growing flock. Plus, I endeavored to be a loving husband and attentive father of two little girls. My doctor warned me that I had the beginnings of a duodenal ulcer. "Relax a little," he said. "When?" I replied.

I finally realized that the problem was not spiritual weakness but human capacity. I didn't have enough physical and emotional energy to expand my ministry *and* grow in my newspaper career *and* care for my young family. If you are in this situation, you know what I am talking about.

Now multiply that by a gazillion mini-locations around the world where dedicated (and tired) laborers are building careers, caring for families, and leading ministries. I have observed that volunteer led outreach ministries grow to about twenty or thirty and then plateau if there is no *full timer* with time and capacity to plan, organize, and shepherd the flock. Of course, there are exceptions.

I love volunteer led ministries. They *are* the key! But without full timers coming alongside, many conventional income 'volunteers' burn out or quit, and their ministries level off.

How many ministries today have plateaued or declined because they are missing full time ministry workers with time and energy to plan, lead, listen, and shepherd?

Volunteer leaders don't have "stare at the wall time." You cannot expect them to race from job to ministry to family over and over and still deliver fresh manna to hungry people. Working harder is not the answer. Sooner or later gifted full time leaders must be added to the ministry team.

In some cultures gift income laborers are illegal. Fair enough — BAM is the likely alternative. But in any culture conventional income leaders will eventually become overloaded. Adding additional volunteer leaders helps, but eventually they, too, need help. Somehow alongsiders must be found to serve the growing work.

The *either-or* question of conventional income workers *versus* gift income workers is a false dilemma. *Both are needed.*

But how do we organize for maximum growth? I am grateful to The Navigators International Executive Team for providing a framework of four types of ministry workers. Which ones are needed in your work now?

Type of Kingdom Worker and Their Funding Method

- *Pioneers: Best funded through gift income*
  Gifted to start new things. Especially for campus, military, and startups.

- *Local Laborers: Best funded through a conventional job*

Lay laborers embedded in the culture go where full time people cannot go.

- *Local Leaders: Best funded through gift income or conventional job*
  Shepherd local laborers, facilitate growing ministries.

- *Alongsiders: Best funded through gift income*
  Gifted mobile workers come alongside local leaders and local laborers to help them succeed.

Two categories seem best filled by gift income workers — pioneers and alongsiders. The categories of Local Leaders and Local Laborers seem best maximized by conventional income workers. Obviously, there are exceptions.

To those who want an 'organic movement' *without* gift income people and *without* administrative structure, I remind you that churches of Paul's day *quickly identified gifted pastors and paid them*. They had a structure and it didn't take long. Paul advised Timothy that:

> *The elders who rule well are to be considered worthy of double honor [remuneration], especially those who work hard at preaching and teaching. (1 Timothy 5:17)*

To back up his admonition to pay them well, he quotes Deuteronomy and Jesus:

> *For the Scripture says, "You shall not muzzle the ox while he is threshing," and "The laborer is worthy of his wages." (1 Timothy 5:18)*

The early church exploded in growth. Teaching pastors were soon identified and paid well. Some think that the "double honor" phrase merely refers to honorific tributes, but the word *timao* is a financial word. Also, the context insists on a financial interpretation.

Also, in Galatians Paul advises paying those who teach:

> *The one who is taught the word is to share all good things with the one who teaches him. (Galatians 6:6)*

Finally, if full time workers were not essential to the growth of the gospel, why would Paul make such a thorough defense in 1 Corinthians 9 of the right for ministers to receive support? Note especially verse 14: "So the Lord directed those who proclaim the gospel to get their living also from the gospel."

Let's be clear — it is not either/or. We need *both* conventional income workers *and* gift income workers. My pastor will never touch the lives of his parishioners' skeptical officemates downtown. But parishioners need an 'alongsider' (pastor in this example) who has capacity to serve the growing fellowship.

If you serve in a country that does not allow gift income workers you must creatively figure out how to meet your Christ followers' need for alongsiders. Don't give up.

Perhaps Jesus' model can help those called to gift income ministry.

Jesus' funding model is reproducible. Luke 8:3 names three of his giving partners: Magdalene, Joanna, and Susanna plus "*many* others who were contributing to their support out of their private means." These three (and many others) had been touched by Jesus and now wanted to help reach still others. That is transcultural.

Someone recently told me that being supported from giving partners is old paradigm. I replied, "You're right. It *is* old paradigm. It's about 2,000 years old. Even Jesus did it."

If God calls some of your workers to gift income ministry, His funding team model will work for them, even if they can't turn water into wine! They needn't copy other countries, but in culturally sensitive ways they can develop giving partners who love supporting their ministry month by month, year by year.

TAKEAWAY

- Have ministries under your leadership plateaued? Is it possible God would call one of the leaders to become an alongsider and be funded by the others?

- Are you failing to penetrate the culture with the gospel by relying on gift income workers only? Perhaps it is time to try a BAM strategy.

- What is preventing both BAM and gift income workers from working harmoniously in your culture?

- Are people in your ministry being called to full time ministry but hesitate to say yes because your ministry has no history of gift income workers?

  - Don't abandon them to solve this issue alone. Get them started in a Bible study on fundraising from my earlier book *Funding Your Ministry* at Navpress.com.

  - Don't merely sponsor a pie supper. Help them develop a wise funding strategy. This is your problem too.

  - Infrastructure is needed. How can giving partners in your culture give to support this 'full time' worker? Pocket to pocket giving is not wise. Who can help you set up an infrastructure of helping donors give without difficulties?

Final Word

NOW THAT YOU'VE MADE IT TO the end, browse through these pages again, prayerfully asking God to speak to you. I hope you will soon do a thorough study of the six fundraising biblical leaders for your own depth of thinking (available on scottmorton.net).

I am confident God will speak powerfully to you during your meditations. The gospel is at stake.

As I said when we began, the remedy for removing funding blind spots is not merely getting more fired up about money or working harder. Instead, think more biblically about how you lead in financial matters.

Though this would be a good place for an inspirational story, instead I give you a six-point application list — not 37 things you might do, but only six. As you have prayerfully meditated through what you have read, what are three immediate action points you cannot postpone, small things you can implement this afternoon?

The second three point application list is for long term action that requires you to connect with your team, your board, your spouse or to spend time alone with God to sort things out.

Getting your action steps in front of you on your screen or on paper is the first step. God will guide you. You can avoid leadership fundraising blind spots.

Immediate Action Steps:

1. _____

2. _____

3. _____

Long-term Action Steps

1. _____

2. _____

3. _____

ENDNOTES

1. Berendt, Robert J. and Taft, J. Richard. *How to Rate Your Development Office: A Fundraising Primer for the Chief Executive.* The Taft Group, 1983.

2. Barclay, William. *The Letters to the Corinthians (The New Daily Study Bible).* Westminster John Knox Press, 1956.

3. Wright, Christopher. *The Gift of Accountability.* Hendrickson Publishers, 2013.

4. Nouwen, Henri J. M. *A Spirituality of Fundraising.* Upper Room Books, 2011.

5. Stewardship. "Our Christian Worker Survey: The Results." *stewardship.org.* 2 Aug. 2011.

6. Harrison, Bill J. "Should Your CEO Be Involved with Fundraising?" *Nonprofit World* vol. 14, July/August 1996: 13-16.

7. 501 Videos. "A donor's gift of $10,000 worth of advice." *moviemondays.com.* 13 Feb. 2013.

8. Berendt, Robert J. and Taft, J. Richard. *How to Rate Your Development Office: A Fundraising Primer for the Chief Executive.* The Taft Group, 1983. ix

9. *ibid. xi*

10. Nouwen, Henri J. M. *A Spirituality of Fundraising.* Upper Room Books, 2011. Page 6

11. Kaiser, Walter C., Jr. *Malachi: God's Unchanging Love.* Baker Book House, 1984.

FAQs About Leadership and Fundraising

Q. As a CEO I feel my development team is not delivering cash large enough or fast enough. What can I do?

A. Have you told your Development Director? Does he realize he is falling short of your expectations? That may be only partially his fault. "If the trumpet [you] gives an uncertain sound..." (1 Corinthians 14:8).

Try this: Ask your development team to write down *what they think* are the top five organizational priorities in funding with a funding goal for each one — a number. You also write your top five and compare. That will help you sort out where you are missing one another.

Q. As a supervisor with field staff who raise support, I sense my team members have stopped dreaming. They say they want to expand their ministries, but nothing happens. Is money behind this?

A. Perhaps. Gift income staff are first concerned about their own support. Don't expect poorly funded staff to raise money beyond their local budgets.

But you can help them. Create a *team expansion budget* and roll up your sleeves to raise it together. This will force discussions about their support — which is good. Leading in funding is part of your job. Do not leave your staff alone to figure out how to expand without your help in resourcing.

Q. How do I help my staff find more potential donors? They have 'run out of contacts.'

A. If they are called to gift income ministry help them see that God has already or will soon sovereignly bring potential partners into their worlds. Advise them to:

- Follow Jesus' example. Those he ministered to supported Him.

List *everyone* who has been touched by your ministry — deeply or slightly. Appeal face to face or Skype to Skype.

- How many names in your cell phone? Hundreds! These phone numbers represent people who, by God's providence, are in your world. Select 25 for the "Appendix A: Top 25 Potential Partners" and add them in. Don't ask, "Will they give?" Ask instead, "Which precious people in my contacts list need to hear my story?"

- Social media. Many staff don't include their 540 Facebook friends as potential giving partners. Maybe not every social media name belongs on your mailing list, but most do!

- Networking. Select a current donor who is a 'door opener' and ask: "Will you do one more thing for me? Will you introduce me to a friend of yours who needs to hear my story?" Your donor sets the appointment with his friend to meet you for breakfast to talk about your ministry dreams and funding. Do it again and again. You buy the breakfast.

- Ask your veteran staff two questions:
  1. How many on your mailing list?
  2. How many of these have you asked face to face in the past three years and who told you 'no'?

  Subtract #2 from #1. That gives the number of people who are still waiting for you to talk to them. Can you find 25?

Q. Fundraising exhausts me. In addition to raising my local support, I'm supposed to do national fundraising, but I'll never survive. What am I missing?

A. Great question. Henri Nouwen, the late mystic/writer said,

> *"If we come back from asking someone for money and we feel exhausted and somehow tainted by unspiritual activity, there is something wrong."*[10]

Years ago fundraising exhausted me, but I had a *money conversion.* Something changed inside me about money! Once I discovered from Numbers 18:21 that God is the Source and therefore giving and receiving are vertical rather than horizontal, the pressure dissipated. Fundraising is a gospel issue, a spiritual ministry, and it is not about me.

May I be candid? Is there too much of *you* in the process? Do you view money as evil? Therefore, seeking it is also evil? And do money worries occupy too much of your soul and are manifested in fundraising exhaustion. Don't ignore what you feel. Something is going on in your view of God.

On the other hand, it could be as simple as your use of time. Conscientious leaders tend to get tired. Green Bay football legend, Vince Lombardi, said, "Fatigue makes cowards of us all." You are not a coward, but physical over-extension contributes to emotional fatigue, which makes fundraising overwhelming.

Q. I prefer to raise money for others rather than for myself. Is that wrong?

A. Many leaders say this, and some even think it is a sign of piousness — it's not.

To leave this feeling behind, you must understand that your fundraising appeals are to advance the Kingdom — no matter if you are appealing for your ministry account, another staff, or a corporate budget. No matter into whose ministry the money flows, it is still not yours! Haggai 2:8 says, "The silver is mine, the gold is mine, says the Lord."

But now let's deal with emotions:

- Do you secretly feel you are *not worthy* of donor dollars?

- Do you fear donors asking how "their" money is being spent?

- Do you fear you can't show "results?"

When someone asks *you* for support, do you chastise them because they are asking *for themselves*? Give yourself the same grace you give others.

Final thought: If you struggle to appeal *for yourself,* ask: "Do I believe my ministry role is truly important?" You understand better than anyone what you do, and I hope you are passionate about it. Why wouldn't you want "that role" fully funded?

Q. How can I help my organization develop more of a biblical fundraising culture? It seems like funding is always an afterthought.

A. Here are five suggestions:

1. Include fundraising in your organizational metrics. It is not unspiritual to count — Moses gave us the book of Numbers! However, metrics are not an end in themselves. While metrics don't provide solutions, they do provide data from which you can ask questions to understand your current reality. Here are four metrics to monitor (See Appendix F, National Funding Progress Report for a thorough metric report on leadership funding):

    a. Number of donors annually. Few national leaders know this.

    b. Support raised by each staff compared to budget.

    c. Corporate donor income (excluding staff) for general or office, special projects, capital campaigns.

    d. Percentage of donor income generated within the country compared with donations received from outside. Unless your work is just beginning, most of your funds should come from within.

2. When I visit staff workers, I always ask the Four Ms — how is the:

    -   Man (or woman)

    -   Marriage

    -   Ministry

- Money (be specific — if you get evasive answers, ask his or her spouse)

3. Put fundraising on the agenda at every meeting. Ask staff to share their latest appeal or a lesson learned. Lead a short Bible study on a money verse. Share your own fundraising stories.

4. Insist your entire organization continually grow professionally in fundraising. Attend seminars, podcasts, read and study biblical fundraising books. For a start, go to *scottmorton.net* to find Bible studies, answers to questions, and short videos.

5. Every new staff must go through at least three days of fundraising training before they begin ministry.

APPENDICES

In the following pages you will find worksheets you can immediately use with your staff or entire organization. Go to scottmorton.net and download full size worksheets under the Resources tab.

Please don't consider "worksheets" as an unneeded add on. Your staff must have places to put their faith—specific actions to take in their funding. Their biggest act of faith might be to list 25 people who need to hear their story—today! Sure, they could do it without a worksheet, but many will not simply because the tool is not sitting in front of them.

Browse through these worksheets and note the names of your staff who need specific worksheets. Then connect your team members with the tools they need. That's called leadership!

Appendix A: Top 25 Potential Partners

Download full PDF: ScottMorton.net/resources

List below, by faith, 25 people who "need to hear your calling story." They may be friends, acquaintances or referrals. Don't ask, "Will this person give?" Instead ask, "Does this person need to hear my story?"

	WHO	PHONE	WHEN /WHERE MEET	WHAT AMOUNT	CALL BACK	RESULTS	HOW TO COLLECT
1							
2							
3							
4							
5							
6							
7							
8							
9							
10							
11							
12							
13							
14							
15							
16							
17							
18							
19							
20							
21							
22							
23							
24							
25							

Appendix B: Creating Your Personal Giving Plan

Download full PDF: ScottMorton.net/resources

Many believers do not plan their giving in detail. "We just give!" But Jesus reminds us that we are to be faithful stewards as we manage our Father's resources (Luke 16:12). Take this survey before and after you meditate on the passages below. In your opinion...

How much should believers give?

☐ 10% (tithe Malachi 3:10)

☐ 23 and 1/3% (three tithes)

☐ "Till it hurts, man!" (US Hippies, 1960s)

☐ Until you can no longer give joyfully (2 Corinthians 9:7)

☐ Whatever you want, no rules

☐ What you can afford, discretionary monies only

☐ Other _____

Toward what should believers give?

☐ 10% to local church, extra to mission organizations if possible

☐ All to local church, let church decide where it goes

☐ Gospel missionaries

☐ Whatever opportunities you know of when you have money

☐ To those who teach you the Word (Galatians 6:6)

☐ Whatever needs God puts on your heart or you feel joyful about

☐ The poor

☐ Family needs

☐ Other _____

How often should believers give?

☐ Weekly or Monthly

☐ Yearly or quarterly

☐ Spontaneously, whenever you feel like it

☐ Regularly by a plan

☐ After all bills are paid

☐ Other _____

Enjoy meditating on the following passages, keeping in mind the questions above.

How much to give:

Malachi 1:7–8 and 3:8–10 How do these two passages relate to one another?

Luke 21:1–4

2 Corinthians 9:6–7

Luke 18:9–14, Matthew 23:23–24 with Luke 11:42 Is Jesus endorsing tithing for today?

2 Corinthians 8:3 and 7

2 Corinthians 8:10–12

Proverbs 11:24–25

Deuteronomy 16:17

1 Timothy 6:17–19

Question: Paul, formerly a strict 'tithing Pharisee,' taught giving in

Corinthians, Galatians, 1Timothy, and Philippians. What does he say about tithing?

Case Study from Colorado:

Robert was a new believer I met with for Bible study. The pastor of his church preached on tithing, and being sensitive to the Lord, Robert asked me, "Should I tithe? Ten percent feels too high, but the pastor said 'God will make it up.'"

Robert earned $1,100 per month in take home pay. After tithing he would have $990 remaining. His rent was $500 and utilities $100. Other monthly expenses included the babysitter, gas to drive to work, food for the family, clothes, insurance, and school supplies. I wondered if Robert could tithe and also pay his bills.

Two days later I met for Bible study with a gifted stockbroker who earned $250,000 per year. If he had heard the message on tithing, he would give $25,000 and then have to 'eke out a living' on $225,000!

What would you advise Robert about tithing? What would you advise the stockbroker about giving?

Where to give:

Galatians 6:10

James 1:27

James 2:15–17

Deuteronomy 15:7–11

3 John 5–8

1 Timothy 5:17–18 with Galatians 6:6

1 Timothy 5:8 and 16

1 Corinthians 9:14

Romans 15:24

How often to give:

1 Corinthians 16:1–4

Proverbs 3:9–10

Question: Shouldn't giving be spontaneous and led by the Spirit?

Question: What if your family needs help? Should you give them what you intended to give to the Lord?

Practical Suggestion: Each January my wife and I forecast our income for the next twelve months and prayerfully discuss what we think by faith the Lord wants us to give. Giving is a non-optional line item in our monthly household budget. We tell our church and mission workers of our intention to give monthly so they can plan accordingly.

As part of our plan we set aside a generous spontaneous amount monthly. If we don't give it one month, we add it to the next.

If our income drops or increases significantly, we adjust our plan.

Do both — let the Spirit guide you in your planned giving *and* let the Spirit guide you in your spontaneous giving. It's not your money! Haggai 2:8.

PERSONAL GIVING PLAN

Application: 1 Corinthians 16:2 implies giving should be in our thinking weekly. Do you have a giving plan? If married, are you and your spouse in agreement? Use local currency.

Projected income for the coming 12 months: $_____ **Monthly average:** $_____

Total to give monthly: $_____ **Or annually if you prefer:** $_____

    1. By plan: $_____ (amount monthly or annually)

        $_____ Local Fellowship $_____ Missions/gospel advance

        $_____ Family help $_____ The poor

        $_____ Other $_____ Other

    2. By spontaneous decision (as part of plan): $_____ (amount monthly or annually)

Appendix C: Up Till Now Report

Download full PDF: ScottMorton.net/resources

Directions: List each person you've appealed to. Include the date of appeal and type of appeal. When you get their response, list it in the appropriate column. Continue to list additional appeal names at the bottom. As you continue to get responses, change undecideds and retotal. Continue to use this worksheet until you hit 40 names appealed to with responses. Then start a new worksheet.

	TYPE OF APPEAL*	LIST THOSE YOU'VE APPEALED TO/DATE	YES MONTHLY	AMOUNT MONTHLY	YES CASH	AMOUNT CASH	NO	UNDECIDED	COMMENTS/ COLLECTION
1									
2									
3									
4									
5									
6									
7									
8									
9									
10									
11									
12									
13									
14									
15									
16									
17									

* F=Face-to-face; L/P=Letter/phone; G=Group appeal; E=Email or letter only; WO=Walk-on; O=Other

Appendix D: Top Ten National Partners

Download full PDF: ScottMorton.net/resources

Identify below the Top Ten people who:

1. Need to hear about your national vision and strategy

2. With your encouragement and genuine ministry could become financial "anchors" to the national work.

Some may be friends already. Some may be acquaintances or even strangers. They might be giving heavily or not at all. Do not ask, "Will they give?" Ask, "Who needs to hear what God is doing *today* in our nation through our mission?" And allow time to minister to them to help them in their spiritual growth.

	Who	Phone/E-mail	Their Giving Interest	What will you ask them to do?
1.				
2.				
3.				
4.				
5.				
6.				
7.				
8.				
9.				
10.				

"Our desire: Every donor a Christ-centered laborer!" *(Matthew 9:36–38)*

— **Lorne Sanny**, Former International Director, The Navigators

"How much are Christians supposed to give?" I asked an Evangelical friend as we walked to a crowded meeting where an offering would soon be taken. He didn't hesitate. "Giving? Ten percent to the church and any extra to the parachurch," he blurted confidently.

"Where did you learn that?" I queried.

"Isn't that what the Bible says?" he responded.

Hmmm.

During a funding seminar in Asia I asked, "How much should a Christian give?" A senior woman leader piped up confidently with the well-worn quip, "The tithe is the Lord's." Everyone nodded. Except me. Looking her in the eye I said, "So the rest belongs to you?" She smiled awkwardly, but she got it. This is the unintended consequence of teaching tithing — ten percent is the Lord's and ninety percent is mine!

I'm not suggesting we water down our giving, but let's remember that tithing is an Old Testament teaching. The New Testament overrides it. Set aside your emotions for a moment and let's see what the New Testament actually says about tithing.

Jesus's words about tithing are brief — only two comments. In Matthew 23:23 (Luke 11:42), Jesus criticized the Pharisees for neglecting justice, mercy, and faithfulness in their tithing. Look carefully at His words:

> *"For you tithe mint and dill and cumin, and have neglected the weightier provisions of the law: justice and mercy and faithfulness; but these are the things you should have done without neglecting the **others**." (emphasis mine)*

To be sure, they were tithing but with the wrong attitude — sans justice, mercy, and faithfulness. *Others* is plural in the New American Standard Bible and it refers to the Old Testament laws — not only tithing! He wants the Pharisees to be good Jews — don't neglect Jewish laws! But He says in verse 24 they are "straining out a gnat and swallowing a camel." Wrong priorities.

This cannot be construed as Jesus advocating tithing for the new Way He is announcing in the gospels.

Jesus also mentions tithing in Luke 18:12 where a Pharisee boasts, "I fast twice a week and give a tenth of all I get." This is not an endorsement!

What about the Apostle Paul? As a former Pharisee, we would expect him to advocate tithing. But when Paul teaches giving (1 Corinthians 16:1-4, 1 Timothy 6:17-19, 2 Corinthians 8-9, Galatians 6:6) he does not mention the T-word.

Why not? Obviously, Paul did not want new Gentile believers to be tempted by Judaism legalities. When the famous Jerusalem Council of Acts 15 met to decide if the Gentiles had to adhere to Jewish law, the answer was no and that included tithing. Furthermore, neither Peter nor John nor James mention tithing in their letters.

If the New Testament is silent on tithing, does it offer a different teaching?

Yes. It's tucked away in Luke 21:1-4, the familiar story of Jesus observing the rich men and a poor widow putting their gifts into the treasury. Jesus said the widow "put in more than all" even though she gave only two small copper coins. Why? Because "she [gave] out of her poverty [her living]" whereas the rich gave "out of their surplus" (NASB). Jesus commended the widow because her giving affected her lifestyle. If we give only out of our discretionary income, we've missed the point.

What about Paul? Paul exhorted Christ followers to abound in generosity (2 Corinthians 8:7, emphasis mine):

> *"But just as you abound in everything, in faith, and utterance and knowledge and in all earnestness and in the love we inspired within you, see that you **abound** in this gracious work [giving] also."*

C. S. Lewis put it well when he said, "I'm afraid biblical charity is more than merely giving away that which we could afford to do without anyway." (my paraphrase)

Is ten percent a good place to start? Certainly for many. Pastors can advocate that, but they cannot say that is what the New Testament teaches.

Now, *where* shall I give? Here's a second misunderstanding: You must give the first ten percent to your local church. Commonly known as *storehouse tithing*, this teaching comes from (Malachi 3:10, emphasis mine):

>   *"Bring the **whole** tithe into the storehouse."*

Not a partial tithe, but all of it.

Malachi 1:7–8 provides the context, and it has a humorous twist. Rather than sending the best of the flocks to Jerusalem, the Jews were sending the worst, those that would probably die anyway. Malachi then asks if the civil governor would "receive you kindly" for giving lame lambs. Absolutely not! That's why Malachi emphasized the "whole" tithe. The Jews were "keeping the law" but they gave their worst, not their best.

Note the word storehouse. Many say this means the local church. These *storehouses* were built in the days of King Hezekiah 300 years previous because the people were so generous in support of the Levites that they ran out of room in the temple. So they built granaries, storehouses, for the tithed grain.

Is the local church the cultural equivalent of the Jewish temple? Does storehouse = church house? Walter C. Kaiser, in *Malachi: God's Unchanging Love* says, "We must be careful about using this verse to insist on 'storehouse' tithing...the storehouse is not equated with the local church."[11]

A pastor friend says asking for the first ten percent for the local church is a "fine policy, but you can't get that from Malachi 3:10."

In my opinion, a significant portion of your giving should go to your local church, where you are being taught, not because of Malachi 3:10 but because of logic. Galatians 6:6 exhorts believers to "share all good things with the one who teaches." If the parishioners don't support their local assembly, who will?

Biblically, where else might we give? New Testament examples include the poor (Galatians 2:10), orphans and widows (James 1:27), missions (Philippians 4:10–20). Give where you choose. Paul summed it up in 2 Corinthians 9:7: "Each man should give what he has decided in his heart to give."

Won't this kill support for the local church? No. Not if giving is taught as a part of discipleship. Too often we talk about money only when we need it.

Why is a correct understanding about tithing important for leaders? Many people around the world are under the law to tithing and at the same time, many believers around the world barely give anything at all. This popular tithing teaching might be well intended, but it is not discipling our people. Something must change, and it is the teaching that is suspect.

So what can be substituted for tithing as the standard for how much a Christian should give? My suggestion is taken from Luke 21:1–4, where Jesus observed the widow and rich men giving.

Give in such a way that it makes a difference in your lifestyle.

Like the widow who gave two small coins "out of her living," give out of your lifestyle, out of money you live on, not merely your surplus. Your generosity should affect the way you live! That may be more or less than 10 percent. You are free. Abound in giving!

TAKEAWAY

1. What do you believe about tithing?

2. What are you teaching about giving?

Appendix F: National Funding Progress Report

Download full PDF: ScottMorton.net/resources

See instructions on following page for details on completing this worksheet.

(A.) NATIONAL FUNDING PROGRESS REPORT
In-country gifts only (local currency)

STAFF INCOME

(B.)Staff names	(C.)Monthly Average (D.)Jan – Dec ____	Monthly Avg Jan – Dec ____	Monthly Avg Jan – Dec ____	Monthly Avg Jan – Dec ____	(N.)Mo Bgt
1.					
2.					
3.					
4.					
5.					
6.					
7.					
8.					
9.					
(E.)Subtotal Staff-Income Monthly Average					

(F.)OFFICE DONATION INCOME

Office – General					
National Projects					
(G.)Subtotal Office Income Monthly Average					
(H.)Grand Total In-Country Monthly Average					
(I.)#In-Country Donors/Year					
(J.)# on National Mailing List					
(K.)Annual Income from Outside					
(L.)Annual Business or Non-donation Income					
(M.)% Donation/Non-donation					

A. This template gives a "high altitude" overview of the financial health of your work and should be compiled biannually or annually. It enables you to "know well the state of your flock" (Proverbs 27:23). All income is from within the country except for Line 18. Instead of a nation, you can use this template for a region or city. If your organization is not capturing this information, suggest they start. B. If you have more than 9 staff with funding accounts, add extra lines or create a page two.

C. Figures are "Monthly Average" except for lines I, J, K, and L.

D. Insert the year beside Jan – Dec at the top. It is important to include figures for the year prior to the initial fundraising training your staff have received. This is your "baseline" to determine if the training is effective and to rate progress. Enter fiscal year figures if you prefer.

E. Subtotal Staff Monthly Donor Income Average. Total your staff monthly averages.

F. "Office Donation Income" income includes general or project giving—any donation not designated for staff.

G. Add "Office-General" and "Special Projects."

H. Grand Total In-Country Monthly Average. Add lines E and G.

I. In-country individuals who gave in the last year one or more gifts. This is your "donor base."

J. Number of people on your database to whom you send (or could send) mailings—donors, former donors or non-donors. This is the broad list of people to whom you send information of any kind—even "in-actives." Generally, aim for 3-4 non-donors for every donor on your list. Don't make the error of mailing to donors only and thereby fail to cultivate future giving partners.

K. Annual Income of any kind received from outside the country.

L. Business or non-donation income includes money generated by business, investments, fees, etc. Pioneer ministries in developing countries must begin with most of the funding from outside (K).

To help your people learn to give generously as part of discipleship I recommend these benchmarks:

    a. Donation income from within the country—60%
    b. Gifts from outside the country—20%
    c. Business, investment or fee income—20%

M. Calculate the percentage of donation versus non-donation income.

N. "Monthly Budget"—last column on the right. Use current-year budget. I have not made a column to create a percentage of income-to-budget because that is not as useful as working in actual amounts above or below budget. But you could easily create that if helpful.

Appendix G: Project Pyramid

Download full PDF: ScottMorton.net/resources

Project Title: _____ Amount: _____

# Major Donors	Could Ask (names)		Amount in each pyramid section

Total Major Donors Needed

Total amount:

Other smaller donors via direct mail or events: no more than 20 percent total needed.

Directions:

- Identify a name for your funding project and the exact amount you need to raise.

- Experiment (in pencil) with differing amounts in each pyramid to reach the total amount needed.

- Insert the name of potential donors into the blanks on the left. You will need two to three names for every gift required.

- Your top 10–15 donors should fund 60–80 percent of the project.

- Don't ask, "Will they give that amount?" Ask, "Is there any reason I could not invite them to give that amount?"

Rethinking Your Financial Values

1. What positive financial values did you learn from your parents? Any negative values?

2. How to become poor: How to become rich:

   10:4 _____   3:16 _____

   14:23 _____   10:4 _____

   20:4 _____   11:24–26 _____

   21:5 _____   13:4 _____

   21:17 _____   14:23 _____

   22:16 _____   28:27 _____

   23:21 _____

   28:19 _____

   29:3 _____

3. Better to have _____ than wealth.

   10:22 _____   22:1_____

   6:16 _____   28:6 _____

   17:1 _____   31:10 _____

4. Meditate on 1 Timothy 6:9–10; 17–19

   Observations:

5. Application: What two main things stand out to you from this study?

A. _____

B. _____

If extra time:

Deuteronomy 8:17–18

Proverbs 22:7

Proverbs 31:24–25

1 Chronicles 29:2; 14–16

Proverbs 23:4–5

Ecclesiastes 5:10–11

Psalm 37:21

Proverbs 27:23–24

Haggai 2:8

Proverbs 6:6–11

Proverbs 30:8–9

1 Thessalonians 4:12

Find more books like *Blindspots* at
CMMPress.org

Living outside of the U.S.?
Contact us for international printing needs.

Fun, interactive, and team-driven

support raising training.

SRS Bootcamp™

You'll be equipped with a real plan, hands-on experience, and the resources to get to your ministry assignment quickly and fully funded.

Register today!

SupportRaisingSolutions.org/Bootcamp

Creating a fully
funded ministry
doesn't happen
overnight.
**We're with you
every step of
the way.**

1. SHAPE YOUR CULTURE

Create a healthy support raising DNA in your organization by discovering powerful building blocks that grow long-term, robust fundraising vitality among your staff.

2. BUILD STRUCTURE

Construct a framework of essential policies, principles, practices, and personnel to effectively organize and guide your staff to consistently thrive in their support raising.

3. ELEVATE TRAINING

Identify the tools, resources, and strengths you need to take your support raising instruction to a new level. Sharpen your skills by learning from other experts.

4. MULTIPLY COACHING

Develop a proficient cadre of knowledgeable and caring support raising mentors at every level of your organization to get your staff fully funded–and stay there!

Join today!

SupportRaisingSolutions.org/network

Free resources

equipping you to stay

FULLY FUNDED

wherever God's mission

leads you.